◁ ▯ W9-BOL-982

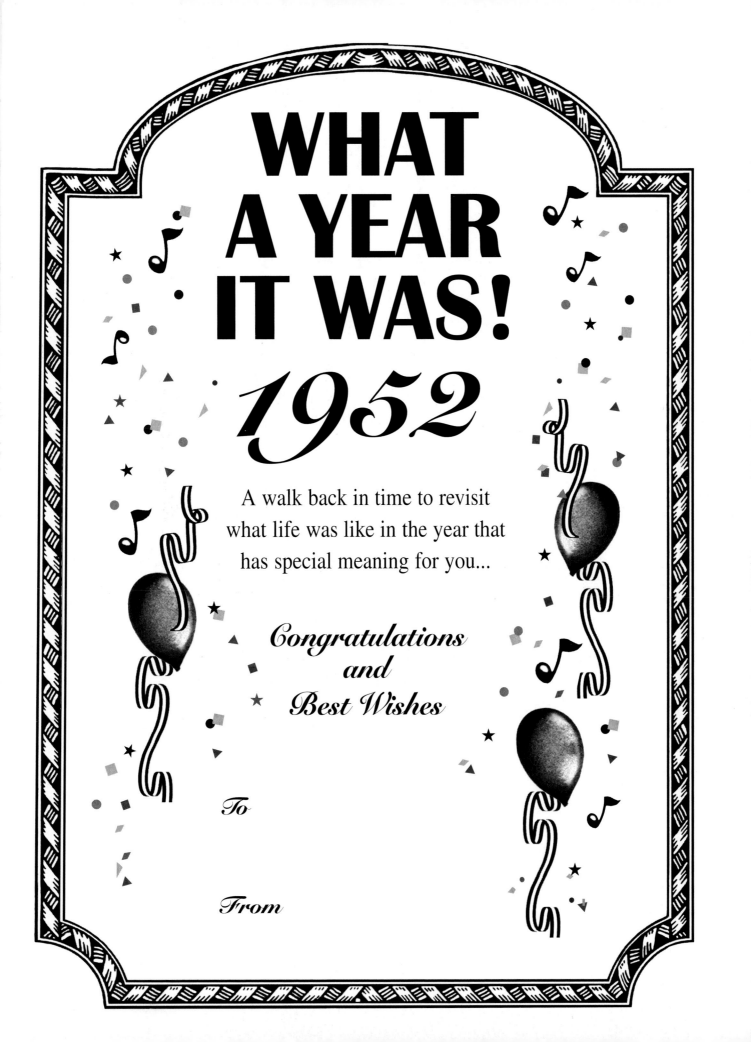

WHAT A YEAR IT WAS!

1952

A walk back in time to revisit
what life was like in the year that
has special meaning for you...

*Congratulations
and
Best Wishes*

To

From

DEDICATION

To My Son-In-Law Michael Rosenthal

You are the son-in-law every mother dreams of
a wonderful husband to my daughter Laurie
an incredible dad to my grandson
and a very special friend to me

Much love,
Bev

Series Created By • Beverly Cohn

Designers • Peter Hess & Marguerite Jones

Research • Laurie Cohn

Special thanks to Kenny Bookbinder for his invaluable help with the Sports section.

Text and images Copyright ©2001 by Beverly Cohn.
Compilation copyright ©2001 by MMS Publishing. All rights reserved under international copyright conventions. No part of this book may be reproduced or utilized in any form or by any means, electronic or mechanical, including photocopying, recording or by any information storage and retrieval system, without permission in writing from the publisher.
Inquiries should be addressed to:
MMS Publishing, 5429 McConnell Avenue, Los Angeles, California 90066
Printed and bound in the United States

CONTENTS

POLITICS
&WORLD EVENTS

Churchill addresses U.S. Congress

Vice President Barkley *(right)* and Speaker Rayburn *(far right)* welcome Prime Minister Churchill as he arrives to address a joint session of Congress. He emphasizes that Britain seeks help only to play her part in the common defense of liberty.

"I have not come here to ask you for money to make life more comfortable or easier for us in Britain. Our standards of life are our own business and we can only keep our self-respect and independence by looking after them ourselves. It is the policy of the United States to help forward in many countries the process of rearmament. That is why I have come here to ask, not for gold but for steel, not for favors, but equipment. And that is why many of our requests have been so well and generously met. The vast process of American rearmament in which the British Commonwealth and Empire and the growing power of united Europe would play their part to the utmost of their strength. This vast process has already altered the balance of the world and may well, if we all persevere steadfastly and loyally together, avert the danger of a third world war or the horror of defeat and *subjugation* should one come upon us."

1952 United

President **Truman** presents **General Eisenhower** with his fourth Oak Leaf Cluster for distinguished service.

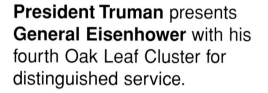

JOHN FOSTER DULLES resigns as Republican advisor to Secretary of State **DEAN ACHESON**

Signings

✔ U.S. signs military aid pacts with **Peru, Brazil, Columbia and Ecuador.**

✔ U.S. signs defense treaties with **Japan, Australia, New Zealand and the Philippines.**

President Truman signs peace treaty granting Japan full sovereignty and officially ending World War II in the Pacific region.

Hailing the Japanese treaty as a step to peace, Secretary of State Acheson commences security talks with Australia and New Zealand.

In his first annual report as Supreme Commander, Allied Powers in Europe, GENERAL DWIGHT D. EISENHOWER declares that the free world is much better able to defend itself this year than last year.

GENERAL EISENHOWER puts in a formal request to be returned to inactive duty presumably to clear the way to run for the presidency ending 37 years as an Army officer.

Admiral Lynde D. McCormick named Supreme Allied Commander in the Atlantic Ocean region.

Supreme Allied Commander General Matthew B. Ridgway is assigned command of all U.S. forces in Europe by U.S. Defense Department.

U.S. AGREES NOT TO LAUNCH AN ATOMIC ATTACK ON SOVIET BLOC WITHOUT BRITISH CONSENT.

U.S. NAVY IS USING GUIDED MISSILES FOR THE FIRST TIME IN WARFARE.

By a vast majority, Puerto Ricans ratify constitution granting them self-government under U.S. control.

WHAT A YEAR IT WAS!

States

With most of the nation voting Republican, there is one noticeable upset in Massachusetts where young John F. Kennedy defeats Republican heavyweight Henry Cabot Lodge winning the Senate seat.

In the New Hampshire presidential primary, Ike beats Taft and Kefauver beats Truman.

Harry S. Truman withdraws from presidential race.

Republican Senator **Wayne Morse** announces his endorsement of Democrat presidential candidate Adlai Stevenson renouncing Eisenhower because of his *"demagoguery, double-talk and dangerous desertion ... of his once-professed political principles."*

Addressing Americans for Democratic Action, President Truman calls the Republican Party the party of *"big business"* that would like to *"turn the country back to the big corporations and big bankers to run as they see fit."*

Addressing a crowd in Detroit, presidential hopeful **GENERAL DWIGHT D. EISENHOWER** pledges that if elected he will go to Korea to seek an end to the war.

U.S. State Department demands that the Soviets give the U.S. monetary compensation for a B-29 bomber shot down off Japan as well as repatriation of any crew members.

William O'Dwyer resigns as U.S. Ambassador to Mexico.

U.S. recalls its ambassador to Moscow, George F. Kennan, following Soviet demands for his removal charging he had made slanderous attacks on the Soviet Union.

... Available for work in the White House.

Democrat from Minnesota **SENATOR HUBERT HUMPHREY** says that he is available for either the president or vice-president nomination.

CANADA

The first native-born Canadian to hold the post, Vincent Massey is sworn in as Governor General of Canada.

1952

The Preside

Democratic presidential nominee Adlai Stevenson and his running mate Senator John Sparkman of Alabama arrive at the White House for a strategy conference with President Truman.

Reporters are on hand to view the new standard bearers of the Democratic Party.

President Truman promises his full support to the Illinois governor and offers to campaign actively on his behalf.

While the Democratic high command confers, General Eisenhower, who has indicated he would accept a Republican draft as the party's nominee for president, gathers in Denver with his political advisors to map Republican plans.

ntial Race

Dwight D. Eisenhower confers with John Foster Dulles who is helping chart a foreign policy course for General Eisenhower and his vice presidential running mate, Senator Richard Nixon.

President-elect Dwight D. Eisenhower chooses three cabinet appointees:

Prior to the election, Nixon defends himself in a television address against allegations that he misused political contributions from wealthy California businessmen. He claims that the money from an $18,000 political fund was used for his expenses in connection with his "fight against Communism and corruption above and beyond my official duties in Washington D.C."

In this same address, he declares that his wife Pat doesn't own a mink coat "but she does have a respectable Republican cloth coat." He goes on to say that he would never return "a little cocker spaniel dog" which his six-year-old daughter Tricia named "Checkers."

Eisenhower assures supporters of his presidential campaign that he accepts Nixon's explanations and tells a crowd in West Virginia: "Nixon is not only completely vindicated as a man of honor, but as far as I am concerned, he stands higher than ever."

Receiving the largest popular vote in history, Dwight D. Eisenhower is elected the first Republican President of the U.S. in 20 years. Republicans gain control of both houses of Congress.

John Foster Dulles,
Secretary of State

Charles Erwin Wilson,
Secretary of Defense

Douglas McKay,
Interior Secretary

Carrying out his campaign promise, President-elect Eisenhower pays a three-day visit to South Korea to promote a settlement to end hostilities. President Truman derides the visit as demagoguery saying that he doubts if either General MacArthur or Eisenhower know how to end the war.

BER
A TALE OF

Conditions can be really rugged in the city of Berlin whose split personality is controlled in East Berlin by the Russians and in West Berlin by the Allied Command.

It looks like the crew bagged a smuggler.

Police of West Berlin check incoming vehicles for contraband. Such measures are necessary to protect the western zone's economy and its German mark.

Here's the contraband – parts of furniture in this false compartment.

WHAT A YEAR IT WAS!

LIN
TWO CITIES

More discoveries are made in the double roof including stockings and bales of textile fabrics.

The smuggled goods are confiscated and added to a mounting collection in the warehouse.

A strange sideline on a city divided between two currencies and two controls.

GERMANY

The Bonn Pact grants West Germany equal status in Europe.

Citing that the neo-Nazi Socialist Reich Party's principles are essentially the same as the former Nazi Party, the West German constitutional court bans that party whose membership is around 40,000.

West Germany signs a treaty with Israel committing to pay $822 million to indemnify Jews for Nazi anti-Semitic acts during World War II. Of that amount $715 million is to be paid to Israel to defray the cost of absorbing refugees from Nazism and $107 million is slated for Jewish organizations as compensation for heirless and unclaimed Jewish assets seized by the Nazis during the war.

WHAT A YEAR IT WAS!

1952 EUROPE

The European Defense Community is formed through treaties signed by the United States, Great Britain, France, Belgium, Italy, Holland, Luxembourg and West Germany.

Foreign ministers of the United States, Great Britain, France and Chancellor Adenauer of West Germany sign treaties restoring West German sovereignty and ending Allied occupation.

BRITAIN

◆ Britain sends 800 troops to Kenya in response to terrorist attacks by the anti-white Mau-Maus and declares martial law.

◆ British Vice Admiral Earl Mountbatten is approved by NATO as Commander in Chief of all Allied naval forces in the Mediterranean except the U.S. 6th Fleet.

◆ **Kwame Nkrumah** named first prime minister of the Gold Coast, British West Africa.

FRANCE

Defeated in the national assembly 341-243, French Premier Rene Pleven resigns.

YUGOSLAVIA

◆ Yugoslav Communist Party congress elects a new 109-member Central Committee which chooses a 13-member executive committee to replace the Politburo with both headed by Marshal Tito.

◆ Border clashes between Italian and Yugoslav troops reported in Trieste.

◆ Yugoslavia breaks off relations with the Vatican.

DENMARK

Danish and U.S. governments disclose the construction of a huge air base at Thule, 930 miles from the North Pole.

POLAND

To help Poland free itself of Soviet domination, Eisenhower calls for repudiation of the Yalta pact.

General Secretary of the Soviet Communist Party,
PREMIER JOSEF STALIN,
calls the first party congress since 1939 to convene to consider reorganization of the party including a name change and the implementation of a new five-year plan.

Headed by Premier Josef Stalin, a new central committee of the All-Union Communist Party elects a 25-member praesidium.

The Soviet government orders foreign diplomats to stay within 25 miles of Moscow and bars them from 22 other cities.

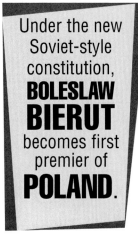

Under the new Soviet-style constitution, **BOLESLAW BIERUT** becomes first premier of **POLAND**.

Russia bars U.S. and British military patrols from part of the superhighway connecting West Berlin and West Germany.

The Soviets in the U.N. Security Council veto the admission of Japan to the U.N. vowing not to admit Japan until American occupation has ended.

Soviet proposal for an armed, reunified, neutral Germany rejected by U.S., Britain and France.

A significant build-up of Soviet military strength in the Far East is reported by General Matthew B. Ridgway.

NATO NAMES GENERAL LORD ISMAY NEW SECRETARY GENERAL.

EMPHASING ITS GOAL TO DETER AGGRESSION, NATO BEGINS NINTH SESSION IN LISBON.

NATO AGREES TO FORM A 50-DIVISON ARMY IN WESTERN EUROPE BY THE END OF THE YEAR.

Described as the largest peacetime naval maneuvers in history, NATO naval forces in the North and Baltic seas launch Operation "Mainbrace."

WHAT A YEAR IT WAS!

1952

KOREAN PRESIDENT SYNGMAN RHEE

President Rhee, just returned to office by an over-whelming majority in Korea's first popular presidential election, reads a citation of honor.

Korean President Syngman Rhee and Mrs. Rhee arrive at 8th Army Headquarters in Seoul.

The occasion is to express his nation's gratitude for the U.S. forces defense of its Asian ally.

As a token of his country's appreciation to America and the United Nations, Korea's Chief of State bestows a high award on General James Van Fleet, 8th Army Commander.

U.S. 8th Army Commander in Korea, General James Van Fleet, is relieved of all routine non-combat responsibilities.

The new commander of U.N. forces in Korea and U.S. forces in the Far East is General Mark W. Clark, who takes over the command from General Ridgway, now Supreme Allied Commander in Europe.

Communist troops in North Korea exceed 1,000,000 according to General Van Fleet, 8th Army Commander.

U.N. truce delegation presents North Korea with Allied terms for truce.

No resolution on the deadlock is reached during the Korean truce delegation's session on repatriation of POW's.

A formal protest is lodged with Communist commanders by U.N. Korean command that U.N. prisoners are being held in camps close to strategic bombing targets in North Korea.

Led by tanks, U.S. troops storm Koje Island POW camp rescuing over 6,800 POW's.

COMMUNIST FORCES LAUNCH HEAVY ATTACKS ON THE KOREAN WESTERN FRONT BUT FAIL TO PENETRATE U.N. LINES.

Five
of the largest hydroelectric power plants in northwest Korea are destroyed by more than 500 U.N. planes.

U.S. BOMBERS LAUNCH HEAVY ATTACK ON PYONGYANG, NORTH KOREAN CAPITAL.

Pummeling the old city of Suan in North Korea with napalm, bombs and machine gun fire, Allied fighter-bombers stage the largest air strike of the Korean War.

Martial law is enforced in southeastern Korea.

U.S. participation in the Korean War passes its **584TH DAY IN FEBRUARY** making its involvement longer than World War I.

1952 U.S. MARINES

A new Bunker Hill makes history that it remains in

This enemy bunker gets hit with grenades followed by a machine gun attack clearing the way for the advancing Leathernecks to close in for the kill.

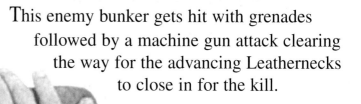

BATTLE FOR KOREA'S BUNKER HILL

as U.S. Marines insure American hands.

As armistice talks continue in a tent in nearby Panmunjom, action flares briefly on this one small sector on the Korean front as a detachment of Marines carries out its assignment to blast out or burn out the enemy's last remaining foothold on Bunker Hill.

Korean truce talks enter their second year with the major stumbling block being the Communist demand for the forcible repatriation of all POW's. Only 70,000 out of 170,000 Chinese and North Korean prisoners wish to return home.

For the moment, the situation is under control.

PASSINGS

Evita, **Maria Eva Duarte de Peron**, beloved first lady of Argentina, dies of cancer at age 33. The one-time actress established a foundation to help Argentina's downtrodden (descamisados), was known for her fancy clothes and jewelry, and was responsible for getting women the right to vote. Her death plunges millions of Argentineans into a mourning frenzy. After her death the city of La Plata becomes Eva Peron, Argentina.

The first president of Israel, Russian native **Chaim Weizmann** spoke over a half dozen languages, was responsible for the Balfour Declaration from England which promised Jews a homeland in Palestine and was an established, groundbreaking chemist before entering politics. Weizmann dies of a heart attack shortly before his 78th birthday.

U.S. SECRETARY OF STATE DEAN ACHESON ADDRESSES SEVENTH SESSION OF POLITICAL AND SECURITY COMMITTEE MEETING OF U.N. GENERAL ASSEMBLY

The spotlight falls dramatically on Acheson as he outlines the U.S. position on the Korean War.

It is a tense Assembly that hears America's leader of foreign policy in a calm and measured tone issue an indictment of Russia's role in the present conflict. During his speech the Soviet Foreign Minister takes copious notes as Russia's good faith on an armistice in North Korea is questioned.

His address is warmly received by a majority of the Assembly and he receives the congratulations from diplomats of the Western bloc.

Once again free nations, along with countries behind the Iron Curtain, face each other before the parliament of nations and calm reason prevails.

United Nations

KOREA

Communist delegation rejects U.N. plan for a man-for-man exchange of Korean War prisoners.

Soviet Foreign Minister Andrei Y. Vishinsky proposes that the U.N. Security Council deliberate on the state of the Korean truce.

Voting to postpone discussion of a permanent settlement of the Korean conflict, the U.N. General Assembly adjourns its session in Paris.

U.N. and Communist truce delegations agree to recommend that a conference be held to discuss withdrawal of foreign troops within 90 days after an armistice and peaceful settlement of the Korean situation.

U.S.S.R. once again rejected by U.N. truce delegates as a neutral supervisor of an armistice in Korea.

China rejects the Indian compromise plan adopted by the U.N. for a Korean truce.

Chinese Communist Foreign Minister Chou En-lai accuses the U.S. of waging germ warfare in Korea.

U.N. General Assembly votes 53-5 to appoint an international commission to investigate Communist germ warfare charges in Korea.

WHAT A YEAR IT WAS!

The 1952 session of the General Assembly convenes for the first time in its new $68,000,000 permanent headquarters in New York.

U.N. Secretary General Trygve Lie announces his resignation to the U.N. General Assembly.

Trygve Lie denies that the U.N. is a Communist nest further denying that the world organization has a policy of firing all U.S. Communists on its staff.

U.N. headquarters in Tokyo reveals that the Soviets have been furnishing military equipment to the Chinese Communists.

ROME

informs Moscow it violated peace treaty by vetoing Italy's admission to the U.N.

Communist charges that U.N. forces have utilized poison gas and germ warfare in Korea are repudiated by U.S. Defense Secretary Lovett.

NO admissions

The Soviets in the U.N. Security Council veto the admission of Japan to the U.N. vowing not to admit Japan until American occupation has ended.

For the third year, U.N. General Assembly bars Communist China.

Communications: Fire instructions received at artillery post. Weight of today's "walkie-talkie" has been brought down to 20 pounds — largely by use of aluminum.

Light, Strong Links for the Chain of Command!

Communication units...the links of the "command chain" ...need the light weight, strength and rustproof durability of aluminum. They need aluminum for non-magnetic shielding, and for the highest electrical conductivity per pound. In shipment, many parts need the protection of aluminum foil...as do rations and medical supplies. The military uses of aluminum multiply...from planes and bazookas to radar towers and walkie-talkies!

And the civilian uses of aluminum multiply no less amazingly. Aluminum for _your_ communications...transmitters, antennas, receivers. And for your home-building...windows, gutters, reflective insulation. More and more aluminum in refrigerators, washing machines, automobiles. Aluminum foil packages on your market shelves. And Reynolds Wrap, the pure aluminum foil, in your kitchen.

Military needs come first, but the goal of today's production expansion is more aluminum for civilian use, too. We face a double job: fighting shortages and inflation while we fight aggression. Reynolds is working at that double job full time, full speed.

Reynolds Metals Company, General Sales Office, Louisville 1, Kentucky.

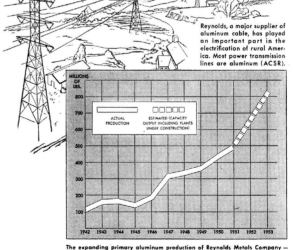

Reynolds, a major supplier of aluminum cable, has played an important part in the electrification of rural America. Most power transmission lines are aluminum (ACSR).

The expanding primary aluminum production of Reynolds Metals Company — a historic chapter in the company's 33 years of continuing growth.

Defense needs limit Reynolds Wrap ...Return Flight Guaranteed!

REYNOLDS ALUMINUM

"The Kate Smith Evening Hour" on Television, Wednesdays—Tallulah Bankhead in "The Big Show" on Radio, Sundays—NBC NETWORKS

YOUNG KING VISITS THE U.S.

17-year-old King Faisal II arrives in New York aboard the Queen Mary for a five-week official visit to the U.S.

The young monarch indicates that his visit is educational and that he is particularly interested in seeing irrigation projects.

But the British-educated king is interested in other things American and one of the first things on his Royal Highness' agenda is a Giants-Dodgers game. And whom is he going to root for? Brooklyn, naturally.

MIDDLE EAST

EGYPT

♦ Egypt is placed under martial law after mobs destroy U.S., British and French businesses in Cairo.

♦ In Cairo, Jordan signs Arab collective security pact.

♦ Naguib cancels the Constitution.

THE ARAB LEAGUE condemns Israel's attempts to restore relations with Germany.

Tunisia

France seizes Tunisian premier and orders martial law.

Death toll rises as French authorities clash with demonstrators in Tunisia over the arrest of nationalist leader, Habib Bourguiba.

Morocco

• Morocco's Sultan Sidi Mohammed requests revision of French protectorate.

• Four killed, 60 injured as Moroccans riot against the French in Tangiers.

Jordan

Declaring him mentally unfit, Jordani parliament deposes King Talal I and proclaim his 17-year-old son Hussein King.

Syria

Syrian government dissolves all political parties and groups.

Iran

♦ Iranian government orders the closing of all foreign cultural institutions outside Tehran.

♦ Premier's aide Hossein Fatemi shot by a Moslem in Tehran.

♦ Iran breaks diplomatic relations with Britain over oil dispute citing Britain's refusal to accept Premier Mossedegh's terms for the nationalization of British oil properties in Iran.

DR. ITZHAK BEN-ZVI is inaugurated second president of Israel succeeding the late Chaim Weizmann.

EGYPT'S KING FAROUK ABDICATES – GENERAL MOHAMMED NAGUIB TAKES CONTROL IN A BLOODLESS COUP D'ETAT

1952

*T*aking control of the Egyptian government, General Mohammed Naguib appeals to the people to beat the first major challenge to his reform program. His newly formed civilian cabinet is the first in Egyptian history to include a member of the Moslem Brotherhood.

The powerful anti-British party defies Naguib when he orders that corrupt leaders be expelled including the popular Aly Maher Pasha, Farouk's Premier.

In reply Naguib tours the congested peasant districts of the Nile Delta and is met with fanatical enthusiasm and unmistakable popular acceptance.

With the capitulation of his opposition, the way is cleared for Naguib's much needed reform program to better the lot of Egypt, one of the world's most poverty stricken nations.

1952

India...

In New Delhi, U.S. signs five-year accord to give India $50 million for economic development.

Jawaharlal Nehru is reappointed Prime Minister of India.

The map shows: Mongolia, China, Korea, Japan, Tibet, Nepal, India, Burma, Laos, Thailand, Vietnam, Cambodia, Philippines, Ceylon

TIBET

Tibetans believe the Dalai Lama is now a virtual prisoner of the Chinese government.

15-year-old Panchen Lama takes office in Tibet with backing from China.

Tibetans riot against famine conditions caused by Chinese Red Army food seizures.

VIETNAM

Communist guerrillas in Vietnam step up their attacks on French troops who are stunned by the death of General de Lattre.

In Vietnam, the French evacuate Hoabinh to mass for Tonkin Delta drive.

According to French authorities a key Viet-Minh division south of Hanoi has been destroyed following a two-week offensive by French and Vietnamese troops.

JAPAN... Allied Headquarters in Tokyo announce the lifting of all restrictions on Japanese production of arms and aircraft.

Cuba 1952

Cuba once again experiences a revolution. The regime of President Carlos Prio Socarras is ended by an almost bloodless coup d'etat headed by former President Fulgencio Batista.

The revolution kicked off at 2:43 in the morning, lasting a little over an hour.

A former sergeant and now general, Batista comes to Camp Columbia, Cuba's key army base, with supporters to address his troops and present his case to his countrymen. Batista says he lost confidence in the existing government.

The new leader says he intends to maintain law and order as a friend of the people until a free election.

In another coup staged in 1933, Batista started a rule of disciplined democracy which lasted for eleven years. Two palace guards are slain and shortly after the deposed president and members of his cabinet take off by plane for Mexico.

1952 ADVERTISEMENT

Only **$270 to London** (above) from New York . . . $486 round trip! It's just overnight by the giant new Super-6 Clippers.

Don't put it off one day longer!

Better hurry, if you want to see Europe this
summer on The RAINBOW at a Clipper*
Tourist fare of $**270**

The demand for tickets on Pan American's new *Rainbow* service to Europe has been tremendous. It saves you up to $125 over the one-way, first-class fare . . . up to $225 on the round trip!

Moreover, Pan American flies you in brand-new Douglas Super-6 Clippers, specially designed for tourist flights. Yes, you go in the world's most modern airliners—flown by regular Flight Crews of the World's Most Experienced Airline! Attractive meals served in flight at low prices.

Better call your Travel Agent or Pan American *right away*.

©Trade-Mark. Reg. U.S. Pat. Off.

$290 takes you to Paris (above) from New York . . . $522 round trip. Similar low tourist fares to every city in Europe!

New book will help you get the most from your trip.
Send for *New Horizons*, big 196-page illustrated book that gives you 13,501 travel facts about more than 900 places on all six continents. Tells what to see, do, wear, buy! Only a dollar. Mail coupon today.

PAN AMERICAN, Dept. NH-17
Box 1111, New York 17, N.Y.

Enclosed is one dollar. Please rush my copy of "New Horizons," postpaid.

Name_____
(please print)

Street_____

City_____ Zone____ State____

PAN AMERICAN
World's Most Experienced Airline

26

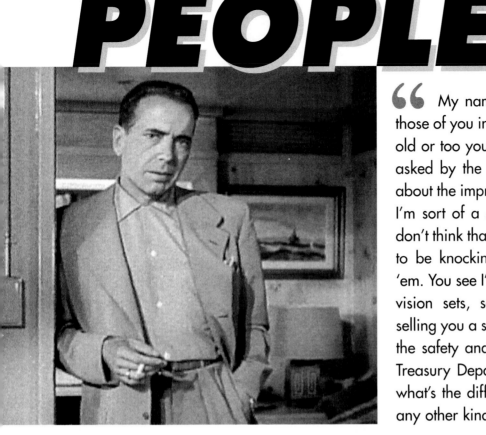

❝ My name is **Humphrey Bogart**, for those of you in the audience who are either too old or too young to know who I am. I've been asked by the Treasury Department to tell you about the improved E Bond. In a way I suppose I'm sort of a salesman. Although I personally don't think that E Bonds need selling. You ought to be knocking on Uncle Sam's door to buy 'em. You see I'm not selling you used cars, television sets, sewing machines, etc., etc. I'm selling you a stake in the future of America and the safety and security of all of us. When the Treasury Department called me, I asked them what's the difference between the E Bond and any other kind of defense bond. ❞

HUMPHREY BOGART PITCHES E BONDS

❝ Now if you'll listen to me for a moment I'll let you in on something. This new improved E Bond pays you three percent. If you hold full time, ten years after maturity, you'll get back twice as much money or almost twice as much money as you put into it. In other words you almost double your dough. Now I think that's a pretty fair proposition. ❞

❝ The United States government stands squarely behind these bonds, now even better. ❞

1952

Eleanor Roosevelt visits Lannoy

Crowds line up in the snow to greet
Mrs. Eleanor Roosevelt who is paying a
sentimental visit to the French town of Lannoy near the Belgian
border, the site of the ancestral home of the Delano branch
of the Roosevelt family.

WHAT A YEAR IT WAS!

Mrs. Roosevelt is greeted by the mayor and other dignitaries.

As part of the welcoming ceremony, the mayor presents her with a document making the widow of our late president an honorary citizen of this small community. He also congratulates her on her efforts for peace and social justice.

Mrs. Roosevelt's next stop is Lannoy Castle, home of the Delano family.

It was from here in the year 1624 that an ancestor of the Delano family left Lannoy to settle on Manhattan Island.

THESE FEET ART MADE FOR WALKING, NOT FOR TALKING

Ava Gardner immortalizes her footprints at Grauman's Chinese Theatre but refuses to discuss her marriage difficulties with **Frank Sinatra**.

☆

HE'LL NEVER AMOUNT TO NUTHIN'

Sonny Bono drops out of Inglewood High School.

☆

Admitting to a reporter that in the past he had very little regard for women, **Cary Grant** says he can appreciate why all his wives divorced him.

A SPECIAL NOTE

A special bill is passed granting permanent U.S. residency to Vienna-born RUDOLPH BING, manager of the Metropolitan Opera, and his Russian wife, Nina.

DO THROW BOUQUETS AT HIM

OKLAHOMA and SOUTH PACIFIC composer RICHARD RODGERS celebrates his 50th birthday.

Albert Einstein blasts the state of college education saying that students specialize too early, are not encouraged in critical thinking and neglect acquiring a *"vivid sense of the beautiful and the naturally good...."* Without these, the student could *"resemble a well-trained dog."*

THE CHEMISTRY JUST ISN'T THERE

Dr. Albert Einstein turns down an offer to nominate him for the Presidency of Israel.

Insisting that her act is straight comedy, GYPSY ROSE LEE is unmoved by the London County Council's ruling to outlaw strip-teasing beginning next year.

THE LADY'S DIARY IS FOR BURNING

MARY ASTOR'S "purple" diary used in her sensational divorce trial is ordered burned by the courts.

Actress GERTRUDE LAWRENCE receives a guest professor "role" at the Columbia University School of Dramatic Arts.

HORSING AROUND ON A SUNDAY AFTERNOON

Suffering from low Sunday school attendance, the Trinity Methodist Church in Los Angeles enlists the aid of ROY ROGERS and TRIGGER to entice the kids into their studies.

THERE ARE SOME THINGS MONEY JUST CAN'T BUY

Saying he wouldn't sell his TRIGGER for all the money in Texas, ROY ROGERS turns down a Texas oil millionaire's $200,000 offer to buy the horse for his 8-year-old son.

LAUREN BACALL and HUMPHREY BOGART produce Leslie, their second child.

Celebrating its 100th anniversary, MARSHALL FIELD'S CHICAGO store invites some former employees to dinner including movie director VINCENTE MINNELLI, (dressed windows) BURT LANCASTER, (floor-walker) ARLENE DAHL (lingerie model) and DOROTHY LAMOUR (elevator operator).

THE LADY IS SINGING THE BLUES

Josephine Baker launches a $400,000 defamation-of-character lawsuit against columnist **Walter Winchell** on the grounds he wrote articles attacking her following an incident at New York's posh Stork Club which refused to serve her.

In a speech given in Buenos Aires on racial discrimination in America **Josephine Baker** says, *"The U.S. is not a free country ... I do not envy those who live there."*

SINGER **PAUL ROBESON** IS BARRED FROM SINGING IN THE OAKLAND MUNICIPAL AUDITORIUM BECAUSE OF HIS POLITICAL VIEWS.

NO WAY OUT OF THE BLACK HOLE

Pope Pius XII predicts that it is completely improbable that man will ever solve the mysteries of the universe.

COOS FOR THE CUBIST

Spanish artist **Pablo Picasso**, creator of the "peace dove" of Communist propaganda, refers to himself as *"only a public entertainer"* and not *"an artist in the great and ancient sense of the word."*

America's primitive painter **Grandma Moses** (91) applies for and receives a social security card for funds to help her in her old age.

SHE STILL WANTS TO BE ALONE

Wearing her signature dark glasses, Greta Garbo is spotted coming down the gangplank of the "United States" after it docks in New York.

WHO YOU CALLING A DUMMY?

Guest star on Edgar Bergen's radio program, movie actress Marilyn Monroe says "yes" to his dummy, Charlie McCarthy, on his marriage proposal.

CAN THIS POOR LITTLE RICH GIRL FIND HAPPINESS?

According to the New York JOURNAL-AMERICAN, the richest girl in the world, Doris Duke, has found peace of mind through the teachings of Hindu Yogi Rao.

Giving Charity A Leg Up

Marlene Dietrich attends the April in Paris charity ball at the Waldorf-Astoria where she displays her famous legs for photographers.

THE PRINCE, THE PRINCESS AND THE BABY

Hollywood glamour queen **Rita Hayworth** receives a "reconciliation" visit from her estranged husband **Prince Aly Khan**, which is upstaged by an unexpected trip to the emergency room after their 2 ½-year-old daughter, **Yasmin**, swallows sleeping tablets.

THE PRINCE AND THE SHOWGIRL

Rita Hayworth and **Prince Aly Khan** announce their reconciliation in Paris.

WHAT A YEAR IT WAS!

The U.S. Court of Appeals in New York unanimously upholds the conviction of underworld czar **FRANK COSTELLO** for contempt of the Senate Crime Committee for walking out of an open hearing last year.

FRANK COSTELLO

Sentenced to 18 months in prison for contempt of Congress, **FRANK COSTELLO** is driven in his private limousine to the courthouse where he surrenders to U.S. marshals. The U.S. Department of Justice petitions for cancellation of Costello's citizenship.

FRIENDS IN HIGH PLACES

A New York crime probe uncovers close personal relationships between Sicilian-born underworld figure **Thomas "3-Finger" Luchese** and leading city, state and federal officials as well as political figures. His U.S. citizenship is cancelled on the grounds he falsified his naturalization papers by failing to report his criminal record.

With Justice Hugo L. Black dissenting, the death sentences of convicted atomic spies **ETHEL** and **JULIUS ROSENBERG** are upheld by the U.S. Supreme Court.

WHY DO I ROB BANKS? BECAUSE, THAT'S WHERE THE MONEY IS

Convicted of bank robbery, **William Sutton** is sentenced to serve two terms of 15 years to life for Sullivan Law offenses not connected with the robbery.

SNUFFIN' OUT THE SNITCH

Arnold Schuster, the snitch who turned in **Willie "The Actor" Sutton**, is shot and killed near his Brooklyn home.

IN THE "STILL" OF THE NIGHT

Churning out 1,000 gallons a day of illegal booze, a still just two blocks from police headquarters in Brooklyn is raided by Internal Revenue Bureau agents.

THE LONG, LONG ARM OF THE LAW

Ralph "Bottles" Capone, brother of the late infamous Al, is indicted on charges of income tax evasion for failing to settle a tax bill of $92,667 for 1922-1928.

WHAT A YEAR IT WAS!

ABOVE: *Nash Ambassador Custom 4-door Sedan. Reclining Seats, Twin Beds, Hood Ornament, glare-free tinted Solex glass and white sidewalls (if available) optional at extra cost. Your choice of three transmissions (including Automatic Overdrive and new Dual-Range Hydra-Matic, at extra cost).*

TAKE COMMAND...IT'S YOUR *Golden Airflyte*

IF YOU DARE TO LET YOUR DREAMS COME TRUE —drive *The Golden Airflyte!*

Here is America's first car styled by Pinin Farina, world's foremost custom car designer. Here are comfort and luxury features so advanced that other new cars seem outdated in comparison!

Here's the supreme thrill of new Super Jet-fire performance—with new horizontal Direct Draft carburetion! (Plus, of course, traditional Nash economy.)

Here is the widest, most comfortable seating to be found in any car . . . the best eye-level vision, front and rear . . . the deepest wind-shield (and new Road-Guide fenders to rest your driving eye)!

Drive the Golden Airflyte, and learn how much *newer* a new car can be . . . how much *finer* a fine car can be . . . how much prouder and happier *you* can be!

Then—if you dare to be envied—make it' your own! Let its possession proclaim your good taste—your refusal to compromise on quality—your keen judgment of value!

For this, the Fiftieth Anniversary Nash, is *your* Golden Airflyte. Take command!

TV Fun—*Watch Paul Whiteman's TV Teen Club. See your paper for time and station.*

The Finest of Our Fifty Years

Nash Motors, Division Nash-Kelvinator Corp., Detroit, Mich.

THE AMBASSADOR • THE STATESMAN • THE RAMBLER

Queen Elizabeth II

THE KING IS DEAD, LONG LIVE THE QUEEN

25-year-old **Princess Elizabeth** ascends to the British throne upon the death of her father, **George VI**, the King of Great Britain and Northern Ireland since 1936, and is proclaimed **Queen Elizabeth II**. The princess and her husband, **Philip**, are in Africa on a goodwill tour when she receives news of her father's passing.

ONCE A WINDSOR, ALWAYS A WINDSOR

Queen Elizabeth II decrees that her children and their descendants will retain the family name of Windsor.

TIME magazine
MAN of the Year
Queen Elizabeth II

LETTING IT ALL HANG OUT

Despite protests from Queen Mother Elizabeth, **Princess Margaret** exercises freedom of choice and wears a gown with a plunging neckline to become the center of attention at Chaplin's *Limelight* world premiere.

Princess Margaret

Refusing to keep quiet during his first Sunday service at Windsor Castle, **Prince Charles**, now the **Duke of Cornwall**, is removed from the chapel by his grandmother.

DOES BABYKINS WANT TO PLAY WITH REAL ROYAL AIR FORCE PLANES?

Heir apparent to the British throne, Prince Charles turns 4.

The **Duke of Edinburgh** turns 31 and gets his first royal 41-gun salute.

THE DUKE TAKES A FLYER

After a month of training at the R.A.F. base at White Waltham, the Duke of Edinburgh makes his first solo flight.

The Windsors

THE DUKE SINGS A SONG FROM "THE KING AND I"

Dressed in a velvet jacket and kilt, the Duke of Windsor entertains his visitors by singing *Getting to Know You.*

THE ONCE AND FORMER KING

The **Duke of Windsor**, formerly **King Edward VIII**, attends the funeral of his brother, **George**, his first participation in a royal ceremony since his abdication for his love, **Wallis Simpson**, now the **Duchess of Windsor**, whose presence is still unwelcome in court circles.

WHAT A YEAR IT WAS!

Emperor Hirohito

Proclaiming his 18-year-old son **Akihito** of age to be heir apparent to the Japanese throne, **Emperor Hirohito** decrees a four-day celebration with rites dating back to the eighth century.

Europe's oldest reigning monarch, Norwegian **King Haakon VII**, celebrates his 80th birthday.

XOXOXOXOXOXOXOXOXOXOX

The **Duke of Edinburgh** matches tic-tac-toe wits with an electronic brain at the National Physical Laboratory in England and loses.

Thailand gets an heir apparent as **King Phumiphon Adunyadet** and his wife **Queen Sirikit** have their first son.

HERE A PRINCE, THERE A PRINCE, EVERYWHERE A PRINCE PRINCE

King Farouk's wife **Queen Narriman** gives birth to a son, **Prince Ahmed Fuad**.

I AM BECAUSE I SAY I AM

King Farouk declares himself a direct descendant of the prophet **Mohammed**.

The Beauty Queens

MISS UNIVERSE
Armi Helena Kuusela
(Muhos, Finland)

MISS EUROPE
Gunzeli Basar
(Turkey)

WHAT A YEAR IT WAS!

Marilyn's Corner

Beautiful movie star Marilyn Monroe is fixed up on a blind date with Yankee slugger Joe DiMaggio.

Marilyn Monroe appears in "Monkey Business" where she is seen for the first time as a platinum blonde.

When studio head Darryl Zanuck finds out that Marilyn posed nude for a calendar, he and other studio executives instruct her to deny that she is the girl in the picture saying that her career will be ruined if she admits the truth. Instead, Marilyn goes before the press and tells the truth and receives an overwhelmingly favorable reaction from the public.

Marilyn seeks legal action against photographer Tom Kelly to stop him from allowing the use of her nude photo on such items as ashtrays and highball glasses.

Marilyn receives more than 5,000 leters a week from admirers with one U.S. battalion in Korea offering to marry her.

FRANK'S Corner

Frank Sinatra's opening at New York's Paramount Theatre is poorly attended.

Flying home to Hollywood to talk things over with his wife Ava Gardner, Frank discovers she and Lana Turner left for Mexico for a little vacation. Lana has been romantically linked to Argentine singer Fernando Lamas but her studio announces that "it's over."

Frank Sinatra's professional life, perhaps a reflection of his battered personal life, hits an all-time low as his talent agency drops him.

1952 Christine Jorgensen

former U.S. Army clerk, 26-year-old George Jorgensen, Jr., creates quite a stir as she returns home to New York from Copenhagen where she had a series of operations transforming her from a boy into a girl.

bombarded by questions from reporters, Christine says she's very happy to be back home and that she doesn't have any plans at the moment, and ends by saying: *"…I thank you all for coming, but I think it's too much."*

FIELDING A PLANE-ING FIELD

RECALLED TO ACTIVE DUTY, FORMER BOSTON RED SOX SLUGGER **TED WILLIAMS** TAKES A REFRESHER COURSE IN FLYING FIGHTER PLANES.

NEW YORK YANKEE OUTFIELDER **MICKEY MANTLE** (21) IS RULED UNFIT FOR MILITARY SERVICE DUE TO A CHRONIC KNEE DEFECT.

FAMOUS BIRTHS / Marianne Williamson / Lorna Luft

HOW SWEET IT IS

Mrs. Richard Nixon announces the winner of Pillsbury's GRAND NATIONAL BAKE-OFF, **Mrs. Peter S. Harlib** who wins the $25,000 prize for her Snappy Turtle Cookies.

GOING TO THE MAT ON THIS ONE

Former wrestler "Man Mountain Dean" decides to run for the House of Representatives in Georgia under his real name, Frank Leavitt.

Adolf Hitler

THE FUHRER'S FAMILY IS FURIOUS

A West German court rules that the last will and testament of **Adolf Hitler**, leaving his estate to the Nazi Party or the state government succeeding him, is valid.

WHAT A YEAR IT WAS!

GENERAL HOSPITAL

Despite surgeons finding a "Do Not Open 'Till Christmas" sign on his chest, 39-year-old comedian **RED SKELTON** undergoes major surgery to correct an abdominal problem.

Clowning Around With Jimmy

Young patients at New York's Bellevue Hospital get a treat when Hollywood's **Jimmy Stewart** entertains them dressed as Buttons the Clown, the character he is portraying in *The Greatest Show On Earth*.

ERROL FLYNN breaks his ankle while filming a movie fight at Universal-International.

+ **Katharine Hepburn** checks into Hartford Hospital in Connecticut on her return from her hit London stage run in *The Millionairess* where her dad, Dr. Thomas Hepburn, is the attending physician.

+ Leader of the Ismaili Moslems, the **Aga Khan** suffers a mild heart attack during a flight to Calcutta, India.

+ Comedienne **Martha Raye** is flown to a Miami Beach hospital after being stricken with a severe intestinal attack while vacationing in Jamaica.

+ **Eddie Cantor** is discharged from a Hollywood hospital where he has been recovering from exhaustion.

+ **Glenn Ford** is thrown from his horse during filming a movie and suffers three broken ribs, cuts and bruises.

+ **Bobby "Emperor of Golf" Jones** is recovering nicely in Atlanta, Georgia following a heart attack.

+ While shooting "Mogambo" in Kenya, **Ava Gardner** picks up a tropical disease.

+ Recovering nicely after an appendectomy, **Marilyn Monroe** is discharged from a Hollywood hospital.

Author **SOMERSET MAUGHAM** (78) is resting well in Lausanne, Switzerland after undergoing a hernia operation.

VERONICA LAKE cancels her summer theatre engagement in Massachusetts due to a virus.

WHAT A YEAR IT WAS!

1952

NOT JUST ANOTHER PRETTY FACE

35-year-old Democrat from Massachusetts, **John F. Kennedy**, *is dubbed the most handsome member of the House of Representatives by 300 Washington reporters with Franklin D. Roosevelt, Jr. coming in second.*

Beautiful socialite **Jacqueline Bouvier** *is engaged to marry John G.W. Husted, Jr. and the wedding is scheduled for June.*

Jacqueline Bouvier calls off her engagement to John G.W. Husted, Jr.

Due to the increasing demands of his U.N. post, **DR. RALPH BUNCHE** resigns as professor of government at Harvard.

Bunche

JOHN FOSTER DULLES resigns as special State Department consultant and Ambassador-at-Large.

Joint Chiefs of Staff **GENERAL OMAR BRADLEY** lists his responsibilities in order of toughness:

1. Official Dinners
2. Press Conferences
3. Pentagon Duty
4. Combat

Despite long hours and abuse, **President Truman** says he likes being president.

President Truman returns to Washington after a 15-day whistle-stop tour across the nation where he visits 24 states making more than 90 speeches on behalf of the Stevenson-Sparkman ticket.

For his moral courage and spiritual leadership, **President Truman** is awarded the International Brotherhood Award of the National Conference of Christians and Jews.

SAILING, SAILING OVER THE BEAUTIFUL SEA

Margaret Truman is among the celebrity passengers on the maiden voyage to Europe of the new ocean liner *United States*.

The U.S. Supreme Court refuses an appeal of the treason conviction of the notorious **Tokyo Rose**.

A JUSTICE FOR ALL

Justice **WILLIAM O. DOUGLAS** receives the first annual Author's Guild Richard E. Lauterbach award for the *"most substantial contribution to the cause of civil liberties."*

WHAT A YEAR IT WAS!

DUH!! JUST KICK ME FOR BEING STUPID

During a House Un-American Activities Committee hearing in Washington, D.C., Representative **Francis E. Walter** calls actor **Edward G. Robinson** *"a No. 1 choice sucker"* of Communist-front groups but also announces that there is no evidence to indicate Robinson has ever been a Red.

Robinson

Hollywood-Broadway writer **Abe Burrows** tells the House Un-American Activities Committee that he was stupid for providing music and lyrics for Communist gatherings in Hollywood but denies being a card-carrying member of the Party.

IF THE SHOE FITS

Head of the Communist witch-hunt, **Senator Joseph McCarthy**, sues **Senator William Benton** for libel and conspiracy after Benton compares him to Adolf Hitler.

McCarthy

1952 ADVERTISEMENT

ON THE GO

. . . every hour of the day and night, America's railroads are busy bringing you the great bulk of the things you eat, wear and use in your daily life and work.

ON THE GO . . . from one end of the country to the other, the railroads are the nation's *basic* carrier of goods—hauling *more* freight *more* miles between towns and cities than all other kinds of transportation put together.

ON THE GO . . . for the future, too, the railroads are improving and enlarging their facilities to serve the nation's needs with even greater efficiency. To make

this continuing investment in America's future, railroads need two things: *materials*, principally steel, for building new freight cars and locomotives . . . and *money* to pay for these improvements. And that money can come only from adequate rates, based on today's higher costs of operation.

Because rail service is a part of every farm, every factory, every business — essential to our everyday life and vital to defense — it is important that the nation's railroads stay strong — able to keep "on the go" for the USA!

ASSOCIATION OF AMERICAN RAILROADS

1952 Coupling

Rhonda Fleming & Dr. Lewis V. Morrill, Jr.

Joan Collins & Maxwell Reed

Rod Steiger & Sally Grace

Artie Shaw & Doris Dowling

Joan Fontaine & Collier Young

Ronald Reagan & Nancy Davis

Betty Hutton & Charles O'Curran

John Drew Barrymore & Cara Williams

Shelley Winters & Vittorio Gassman

Brigitte Bardot & Roger Vadim

Judy Garland & Sid Luft

Tippi Hedren & Peter Griffith

Dick Clark & Barbara Mallery

Larry King & Freda Miller

Tony Bennett & Patricia Beech

Elizabeth Taylor & Michael Wilding

Lil' Abner & Daisy Mae

Jane Wyman & Fred Karger

Vera Ralston & Herbert J. Yates

Mickey Rooney & Elaine Mahnken

Jo Stafford & Paul Weston

Pearl Bailey & Louis Bellson, Jr.

Xavier Cugat & Abbe Lane

Uncoupling

Maureen O'Hara & Will Price

Ethel Merman & Robert Levitt

Agnes Moorehead & John G. Lee

Olivia de Havilland & Marcus Aurelius Goodrich

Franchot Tone & Barbara Payton

Arlene Dahl & Lex Barker

Steve Allen & Dorothy Goodman

Bertrand Russell & Patricia Helen Spence

Gene Tierney & Oleg Cassini

Teresa Wright & Niven Busch

Gloria Grahame & Nicholas Ray

Celeste Holm & A. Schuyler Dunning

Veronica Lake & Andre de Toth

Hedy Lamarr & Ernest "Ted" Stauffer

Clark Gable & Lady Sylvia Ashley

William Saroyan & Carol Marcus Saroyan

Lana Turner & Henry J. "Bob" Topping

Ernie Kovacs & Betty Wilcox

Xavier Cugat & Lorraine Allen Cugat

Lee J. Cobb & Helen B. Cobb

BRITISH PRIME MINISTER WINSTON CHURCHILL CELEBRATES HIS 78TH BIRTHDAY.

In a speech for which she receives a 20-minute standing ovation, **Mrs. Franklin D. Roosevelt** says that while the United Nations is *"not a cure-all"* without it, *"our country would walk alone, ruled by fear instead of confidence and hope...."*

General Dwight D. Eisenhower receives France's highest decoration—the Medaille Militaire—during a formal farewell to Paris as SHAPE commander.

Dwight Eisenhower is made honorary president of the Camp Fire Girls.

The widow of World War II Air Force chief **General H.H. "Hap" Arnold** turns over 15,000 of his personal papers to the Library of Congress.

Self-Realization Fellowship founder and self-realized himself, **Guru Paramahansa Yogananda**, *world-renowned yoga and meditation teacher, has his mahasamadhi (conscious departure of the soul) at age 59, following a speech in Los Angeles. A notarized statement signed by the Director of Forest Lawn Memorial-Park testified: "No physical disintegration was visible in his body even twenty days after death...This state of perfect preservation of a body is, so far as we know from mortuary annals, an unparalleled one...."*

•

A shy and sickly man, **Britain's King George VI** *became King in 1936 when his older brother Edward abdicated after a short reign. Following a long illness, the King dies in his sleep of a coronary thrombosis at age 56. Staying in London while it was bombed during World War II forever endeared King George to his subjects. He also pitched in at an arms plant during the war. Royalty and dignitaries from around the world attend his funeral, and one million of his subjects line the coffin route. He is buried at Windsor Castle, with his ancestors.*

HUMAN — 1952
iNTEREST

JITTERBUGGERS
STRUT THEIR STUFF

Contestants gather in New York for a Jitterbug contest.

These acrobatic hep cats have the floorboards jumping as they show off their best moves.

he'll be *dancing* to a different tune

Spending $1,200 for ballroom dancing lessons is more than the wife of a $200 a month gardener could stand so she files for and is granted a divorce.

WHAT A YEAR IT WAS!

TRAINING TO SKATE DUTCH STYLE

If you stumble upon these Dutchmen in the woods you might wonder what's going on.

*N*o these men are not fugitives from a Russian dance company. These familiar dance movements are just part of their training.

*I*f you think they look like skaters, you're absolutely right. They are skaters getting in shape for the winter Olympics in Norway. It's sort of preflight training. Once their muscles are in tip-top condition, these Dutch champs will take off for a real workout on the ice.

P S S T . . .
WANNA BUY A HOT TYPEWRITER?

Rumania is cracking down on anti-Communist propaganda by requiring a permit to own a typewriter, violation of which is as severe as possessing illegal firearms.

Hurry Up And Bury The STIFF

Rumania has a new law limiting funerals to no more than 45 minutes.

SLAM, BAM, BACK TO WORK

Citing that Hungarian newly-weds are taking an average of two days off for a honeymoon, the Communist government issues an order requiring newlyweds to be back on their factory assembly lines a half-hour after their wedding.

Great Britain abolishes identity cards introduced at the beginning of World War II.

HOW ABOUT JUMPING OFF THE BRIDGE INSTEAD?

The Taipei Hotel Owners' Association issues a request to people contemplating suicide that they please do it outside the hotel as suicides in the hotel cause the management financial and mental stress.

Hey sailor, you wanna have a good time?

Tokyo's "Red Light District" opens, boasting a "working" population of almost 14,000 prostitutes occupying 2,000 brothels.

WHAT A YEAR IT WAS!

LONDON
CELEBRATES SEWING WEEK

What's a haystack doing in the middle of London? Why to hide a needle and to dramatize the old saying.

It's sewing week in old London town and this crowd is ready to find a needle in a haystack.

The guy or gal who finds it wins a brand new sewing machine. So far no luck.

And the winner is Rhoda Selby who receives her coveted award.

Oh - - - The sewing machine the sewing machine, a girl's best friend!

WHAT A YEAR IT WAS!

1952 Exhibition Of Swiss Mechanical Watches And Jewelry

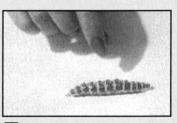

This crawling caterpillar was made 200 years ago. Swiss watchmakers created the intricate miniatures in their spare time.

Children are fascinated with an exhibition of watches and jewelry in Geneva, Switzerland. The mechanical figures rival real life in their amazing actions.

Here's a tiny music box with animated puppets no bigger than your thumbnail.

Among these little gems of artistic expression are carved wood automatons created by makers of cuckoo clocks.

A cobbler and his wife with the little woman appearing to get in the last word.

These chirping birds are so real looking you might be tempted to leave them some bird seed.

But, alas, he's only a wooden bird in a gilded cage.

fund raising with floral fantasies 1952

Oakland, California's Diablos Country Club is the site of a charity event to benefit Children's Hospital.

Floral fantasies created by the Master Florist Association include this "Birds In A Gilded Cage" comprised of more than 500 flowers, taking 37 hours to complete.

This imaginative creation is entitled "Wings Of Fantasy," an appropriate name for this five-foot wide headdress fashioned of carnations.

This peacock contains 1600 chrysanthemums, carnations and orchids.

Every one of these showpieces is stunningly effective including this topical flying saucer.

Spectators enter into the spirit of things and some ornate creations of their own are seen on the sidelines.

As in earlier years, the traditional fundraising ball is a huge success and achieves its purpose of aiding the city's Children's Hospital.

WHAT A YEAR IT WAS!

1952

Canadian sculptor Owen Butler completes his masterpiece, a life-size statue made of butter.

Over 2,000 pounds of fresh Grade A farm butter are used in the sculpture depicting the Queen in her uniform as Commander and Chief of the Grenadier Guards.

A CANADIAN GRADE A TRIBUTE TO
QUEEN ELIZABETH II

Just a final pat or two and the statue is ready for display at the Canadian National Exhibition in Toronto.

One might say it looks good enough to eat and that will be its eventual fate as after the exhibition the Queen will be washed, sterilized and eaten but not before it is preserved in a plastic cast for posterity.

Despite the fact that butter is rationed in England, the statue is considered to be in very good taste.

A ROUND OF TEA FOR EVERYONE!!
After 12 years Great Britain removes rationing of its "national beverage"
– *tea*.

WHAT A YEAR IT WAS!

Something To BARK About

DALE CARNEGIE is named *Dog's Best Friend* by the National Dog Welfare Guild celebrating the 25th anniversary of National Dog Week.

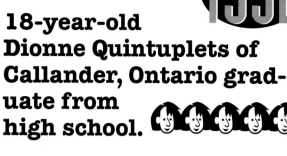

The 10 Most Popular DOGS in America

Cocker Spaniel	Chihuahua
Beagle	Boston Terrier
Boxer	German Shepherd
Collie	Pekingese
Dachshund	Pomeranian

NOBEL · PEACE · PRIZE Albert SCHWEITZER

I Just Have To Have That Pink Feather Boa
A study reveals that one out of every three items purchased by the American consumer is selected on impulse.

THANKS—But I'll Pass On The Cake

The only gorilla to survive 25 years in captivity, Bamboo celebrates this milestone at the Philadelphia Zoo with a birthday cake made of cod liver oil, peanut mash and oyster shell followed by a watermelon chaser.

THE BAHAMAS ESTABLISH THE SOCIETY FOR THE PROTECTION OF THE FLAMINGO.

GET OUT YOUR NOSE PLUGS, WE'RE IN SECAUCUS

With its pig population of 75,000, Secaucus, New Jersey holds the dubious title of the smelliest town in America.

WHAT A YEAR IT WAS!

18-year-old **Dionne Quintuplets** of Callander, Ontario graduate from high school.

THE VAST WASTELAND EXPANDS

A dozen new cities are now part of the national television network including Dallas, Denver, Fort Worth, Houston, Miami, New Orleans, Oklahoma City, Phoenix, Portland, San Antonio, Seattle and Tulsa.

THE WORLD 50 YEARS FROM NOW (PREDICTIONS)

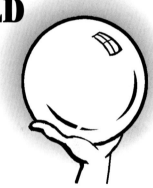

1 Cancer, the common cold and tooth decay will be conquered.

2 Body parts will be regenerated.

3 The Solar System will be explored.

4 A ship will be built that will reach the nearest star.

5 Your personal telephone will be small enough to carry in your bag.

6 Your home telephone will record messages, answer simple queries and transmit images.

7 Communism will not exist.

8 Fish and yeast will become our principle source of proteins.

9 Beef will be a luxury.

10 Lamb and mutton will disappear.

11 We will never have manlike robots with manlike reactions or laboratory creation of life.

U.S. POPULATION PASSES
158 MILLION.

PRESIDENT TRUMAN DESIGNATES SEPTEMBER 17th ANNUAL CITIZENSHIP DAY.

THE BIG SQUEEZE

The "World Atlas" makes the City of **NEW YORK** the world's largest metropolitan area with **8,000,000** people filling its five boroughs.

With alien smuggling being a worldwide racket, the "N.Y. Herald Tribune" reports that 4-5 million aliens have entered the U.S. illegally since the end of World War II.

KEEPING THEM DOWN ON THE FARM

Metropolitan Life Insurance Company releases statistics that show Americans are still predominantly a small-town and rural people despite the rapid growth in city population.

Which Witch is Which?

Despite being rebuked by both Presidential candidates, Dwight D. Eisenhower and his running mate, Senator Richard Nixon, declare that they will support Hitler-like Senator Joseph R. McCarthy if he wins the renomination in the Wisconsin GOP primary.

GENERAL PHYSIQUES OF VARIOUS OCCUPATIONS

OCCUPATION	PHYSIQUE
Scientists	Lean & Muscular
Artists	Portly
Lawyers	Portly
Teachers	Thin
Typical American	Tall, Muscular & Well Proportioned

AVERAGE U.S. MALE

WEIGHT 164 ¾ lbs.

HEIGHT 5'9"

Men whose annual income never exceeds $2,500 have their highest-income year at age 43 or 44 while men in the $5,000 bracket have their highest-income year at 49-50.

Latin America's population is the fastest growing in the world.

A recent Gallup Poll shows that 81% of voters sampled would vote for a qualified candidate even if he is divorced while 14% say they would not.

A Look At What AMERICAN FAMILIES *Have*

Life Insurance 75%
Own Home (non-farm families) 54%
Savings Account 45%

Are You Listening REPUBLICANS??

Key U.S. educators and delegates to the 90th annual National Education Association convention overwhelmingly support separation of church and state and the distribution of public funds exclusively to publicly controlled and tax-supported schools.

Here We Go Loop Dee Loo

According to a study published by the Public Affairs Institute, tax loopholes cost the U.S. Government $4.5 billion a year in lost revenues.

Thanks to a new bill, taxpayers can now deduct 20% from their gross income for charitable contributions instead of the current 15%.

WHAT A YEAR IT WAS!

TRUMAN

564-foot Hungry Horse Dam, third highest in the world, is dedicated by President Truman in Montana.

Way to go, Harry!

The Armed Forces is now authorized to confer commissions on women doctors, dentists and other medical specialists as a result of a bill signed by President Truman.

- President Truman signs a bill giving more authority to federal inspectors to enforce coal mine safety measures.

- The McCarran-Walter Act calling for the tightening of the immigration quota system becomes law as Congress overrides President Truman's veto.

A G.I. BILL OF RIGHTS
is signed by President Truman making veteran benefits available to soldiers who served in the Korean War.

BETTER LATE THAN NEVER
U.S. prisoners of World War II forced to work without compensation or subjected to cruel punishment are awarded per diem pay under a new bill signed by President Truman.

SOCIAL SECURITY
President Truman signs a bill increasing monthly Social Security benefits by a minimum of $5.00 or 12 1/2% – whichever is greater.

THE U.N. HUMAN RIGHTS COMMISSION
approves two measures – one guaranteeing people the right to plan their own destinies, the other insuring protection of their natural resources from foreign exploitation.

YOU LOAD 16 TONS
Congress provides for safer working conditions in coal mines where operations involve interstate commerce.

ALL IN A DAY'S WORK
A law designed to eliminate discrimination against women is passed in New Jersey calling for equal pay for equal work.

Letting It All Hang Out
Overruling an earlier decision in Mutual Film Corp. v. Industrial Comm., the Supreme Court broadens the free speech and free press guaranties under the first and fourteenth amendments to include freedom of expression by motion pictures.

THEY DIDN'T CRAP OUT
Requiring gamblers to buy a $50 tax stamp is declared unconstitutional by the U.S. District Court in Philadelphia.

A CALIFORNIA LAW
forbidding aliens from owning land in California is declared unconstitutional by the state Supreme Court.

1952

U.S. restaurants ordered by Office of Price Stabilization to display ceiling prices for their meals and beverages.

GOOD TO THE LAST DROP

An estimated 16.4 lbs. of coffee will be consumed by the average consumer this year.

HOLY WARS

To give consumers more doughnut, the Donut Institute announces the reduction in the size of the hole from 7/8 of an inch to 3/8 of an inch.

a dentist's dream

With chocolate candy leading in consumer popularity, the candy industry takes in an estimated $1 billion in sales.

SWEET TOOTH HEAVEN

Philadelphia's American Stores Company builds the largest automatic bread and cake bakery in the world boasting a weekly capacity of 2,500,000 lbs. of bread, in addition to capacity for cakes and other sweet goodies.

HUNGER

According to President Truman, in order to win the Cold War, the U.S. must wage war against hunger.

HOOFING IT OUT OF THERE

Chicago's Food Inspection Bureau Chief resigns on the heels of a large-scale investigation of the sale of horse meat labeled beef.

NOT EXACTLY Mellow Yellow

"Operation Oleo" hits New York State as yellow oleomargarine is legally sold for the first time in many years despite vigorous opposition from the farming community to the passage of the bill legalizing its sale.

A family of four spends $1,300 a year for food which weighs in at 2 1/2 tons breaking out as follows:

Milk	.698 quarts
Potatoes	.690 lbs.
Beef	.300 lbs.
Ham	.144 lbs.
Eggs	.131 dozen
Flour	.450 lbs.
Sugar	.350 lbs.
Ice Cream	.8 1/2 gallons

RISING TO THE OCCASION

For the first time in our nation's history, bread will be standardized according to guidelines issued under the Federal Food, Drug and Cosmetic Act.

baa baa
Black Sheep Have You Any Rice
The U.S. rice crop reaches a new record of 47,730,000 bags.

Enrollment in the 4-H clubs for boys and girls climbs to a record high of 2,004,139.

A CHILLING STATISTIC

Strawberries hold the #1 popularity spot in frozen fruits with green peas holding the #1 spot for veggies.

BETTER PLANT SOME MORE
strawberries

For the first time since 1910, Los Angeles loses its first place ranking as the leading farming county in the nation.

With Enough Left Over For Egg On Your Face

U.S. farmers (with a little help from their chickens) produce a record number of eggs totaling over 165,000,000 cases with the average person consuming approximately 412 eggs.

MILKING IT FOR ALL IT'S WORTH

Stepping up to the pail three times a day for 17 years, Pansco Hazel, a Holstein-Friesian cow, is the new champion milk cow of the world, averaging 37 quarts per day.

The Milking Way

Milk production in the U.S. is down slightly over last year at an estimated 114,800,000 lbs.

MILK

KEEP THAT CAN OPENER HANDY

The average person will eat 41.2 pounds of canned vegetables this year.

CAN goods CAN goods CAN goods

1952

IN SEARCH OF JOSHUA
Jericho is excavated.

OK EVERYONE, LET'S PUT AWAY ALL SHARP OBJECTS

Aside from an occasional quarrel where they cut each other's heads off, Indian Prime Minister Nehru tells a conference of Indian anthropologists that he is quite comfortable with India's 26 million primitive aborigines which include head-hunting Nagas, Nilgiri pygmies and dusky Santhals.

Five Roman Catholic priests are arrested in Poland on charges of heading a pro-Western spy ring.

The High Cost Of Freedom

$1,000 is the going rate for a Jewish person to flee Hungary which buys a train reservation and valid exit permit.

With over six million Jews killed during World War II, a census taken in 17 countries by the World Jewish Congress reveals there are only approximately 11,672,000 Jews remaining.

Jerusalem
celebrates the 3,000th year since it became the capital of King David's kingdom.

THERE ARE 2,796 LANGUAGES SPOKEN IN THE WORLD

HE WAS ONLY OBEYING ORDERS
Wilhelm Schepmann is the first ex-Nazi to win elective office in West Germany.

For the first time in any West German court, Hitler's rule of Germany is declared illegal and those who were involved in the assassination plot against him in 1944 are declared heroes, not traitors.

Soviet authorities bar West Berlin residents from the Soviet zone of Germany.

16,000 East Berliners escape to West Berlin during the month of August.

Three U.S. priests are seized as they cross the border into East Berlin.

54

WHAT A YEAR IT WAS!

GETTING EQUAL

Citing unequal facilities, the Delaware Court of Chancery rules that black children must be admitted to mixed high and elementary schools.

🔓 With Baltimore's city council voting 5-3 to change its public school segregation policy, ten blacks are admitted to an all-white school for the first time.

🔓 Former longshoreman Oscar L. Thompson is the first black to get a degree from the University of Texas.

🔓 For the first time, black students are admitted to the graduate school of the University of Tennesee and the dental college of the University of Texas.

🔓 Fisk and Howard universities become first black schools in America to get Phi Beta Kappa charters.

🔓 Florida Supreme Court throws out case involving five black students seeking admittance to the University of Florida on the grounds that equal facilities are available at the Florida A & M College for Negroes in Tallahassee.

🔓 The first black student is admitted into Groton, the exclusive boys prep school.

EISENHOWER warns white Southerners they could lose their rights by not protecting the rights of blacks.

U.S. Supreme Court upholds decision barring segregation on interstate railways.

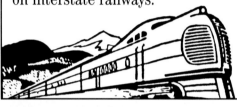

The U.S. Supreme Court upholds a lower court decision that the Atlantic Coast Railroad may not require blacks to travel in "Jim Crow" cars on interstate trips.

GETTING INTO THE SWIM OF THINGS

Citing the city's swimming pool for blacks is inferior, Federal District Judge Albert A. Ridge orders Kansas City's all-white pool be opened to blacks.

HITTING SOME BAD NOTES

Citing alleged bias against blacks in their national membership policies, the UCLA Student Government withdraws recognition from campus chapters of three national music sororities — Mu Phi Epsilon, Sigma Alpha Iota and Phi Beta.

1952 IS THE FIRST YEAR WITHOUT A LYNCHING SINCE 1882 ACCORDING TO TUSKEGEE INSTITUTE.

THE PRICE IS A BIT TOO HIGH TO PAY

After receiving a threatening letter on KKK letterhead, 60-year-old black grocer, C.L.C. Glymph, withdraws from the primary race for town council in Gaffney, South Carolina.

Setting Up Separate Rolls For Black Voters In Cape Colony Declared Unconstitutional By The Appellate Division Of The South African Supreme Court.

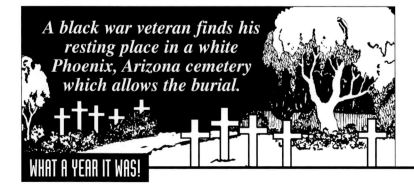

A black war veteran finds his resting place in a white Phoenix, Arizona cemetery which allows the burial.

WHAT A YEAR IT WAS!

PARTY PROFILE BLACK VOTERS
Survey Conducted by the "N.Y. Herald Tribune"

DEMOCRATS	62%
REPUBLICANS	24%
INDEPENDENTS	14%

1952

MOST POPULAR LADIES MAGAZINES

LIFE

WOMEN'S HOME COMPANION

Saturday Evening POST

McCall's

Ladies Home Journal

HAWAIIAN CONGRESS APPROVES BILL PERMITTING WOMEN TO SERVE ON JURIES IN THE TERRITORY.

There she is... The new Miss America is 19-year-old Neva Jane Langley from Macon, Georgia.

- **Washington gets its first female ambassador, India's Shrimati Vijaya Lakshmi Pandit.**

- **Mrs. Beth Campbell Short is appointed White House correspondence secretary becoming the first woman in history to hold that position.**

- **American Mother of the Year: Mrs. Toy Len Goon (57) – Chinese-born laundress living in Portland, Maine.**

Miss Juror

PROFILE OF THE AVERAGE *housewife*

Married 12 Years

Has One Child

Lives In A Five-Room House

Does Most Of The Laundry At Home

Has An Oven With An Automatic Timer *(which she doesn't use)*

Contributes 39% Of The Family Income *($6,290 average)*

(Approx. Number of Working Wives: 10,000,000)

Out Of The Kitchen And Into The Voting Booth

Guaranteeing women the right to vote and to hold office, the U.N. General Assembly adopts an International Convention on the Political Rights of Women.

LET THEM STAY CHILDLESS

Opposing the easing of Britain's divorce laws, the Church of England also recommends that artificial insemination be made a criminal offense.

STILL BAREFOOT AND PREGNANT

An interpretation of the Koran denying women the right to vote or sit in parliament is issued by Al Azhar University in Cairo.

SOCIAL SECURITY

A Dallas federal judge upholds ruling that housewives are required to collect Social Security taxes from domestic help.

JUST IN CASE IT RAINS IN PARADISE

A free consultation in divorce proceedings is a prize awarded by a Hamburg, Germany radio station to the ideal bridal couple.

Spring, When A Cricket's Fancy Turns To Other Crickets

The curator of Chicago's Natural History Museum explains the invasion of black field crickets flooding streets, homes and office buildings is due to the mating season and that the insects are enjoying a "middle-aged fling."

An Australian man

is granted a divorce after he charges that his wife's boy-friend has been sneaking in and out of his wife's bedroom for the last 18 months, beats him up and regularly chases him into the street.

WHAT A YEAR IT WAS!

IN THE EYE OF THE BEHOLDER

	Thinks Spouse Is Good Looking	Thinks Spouse Is Better Looking Since Wedding
Men:	82%	37%
Women:	62%	33%

HIS "LID" STILL SEARCHING FOR HIS "POT"

Divorcing for the 14th time, a 39-year-old Seattle man insists that the right girl for him is out there and vows to continue his quest.

COMING BACK FOR MORE

Most divorced women remarry within five years.

TEN COMMANDMENTS
for ministers' wives
(Southern California Conference of Seventh-Day Adventists)

ah men sister

I Thou shalt have no interests more important to thee than thy husband's.

II Thou shalt not make unto thee any church clique or anything resembling it.

III Thou shalt not take thy husband's name in vain.

IV Remember thy intimate family matters, to keep them secret.

V Honor thy husband by keeping thy place, that his years of ministry in the cause of God may be long.

VI Thou shall not gossip.

VII Thou shalt not be a burden on others.

VIII Thou shalt not appear untidy.

IX Thou shalt not covet a taste beyond thy husband's income.

X Thou shalt not covet thy lay sister's or fellow minister's house, furniture, car or whatsoever thy sister may have.

WHAT A WET BLANKET

A New Jersey woman sues her husband for divorce on the grounds that he objects to her long, hot showers which he claims are running up his gas bills.

GIVING NEW MEANING TO A PERSONALIZED ANNIVERSARY GIFT

A New Jersey judge recommends that a couple separate when the wife testifies that her husband owns a revolver containing a special bullet with her initials on it.

HAMMERING AWAY AT HIS POINT

The judge awards a divorce to a Cincinnati housewife after she testifies that during an argument her husband pounded her wedding ring with a hammer until it was flat as a pancake.

1952 teen speak

PHRASE	TRANSLATION
How's your ear?	Hi
He's on the list	She likes him
Take it away, I'll buy bonds	She doesn't like him
Buttercup	He likes her
Moose or crocodile	He doesn't like her
P.C.	Privileged character as in teacher's pet
Valentino or Fred the Second	A good dancer
The Warden, the Eagle or Mrs. Legree	A strict parent
Flaked-out	Tired
Underwater basket weaving	Easy class
Down Fang	A boy being too aggressive
Let's split a few syllables	Let's talk

The Whirling Twirlers

17-year-olds **Alta Burg** of Red Lion, Pennsylvania and **Tommy Zedaker** of Burghill, Ohio win the baton-twirling world championships.

HOW WE DO
AS THE YEARS GO BY

AGE	DESCRIPTION
20s	Greatest learning capacity
25-35	Big personality changes
55-56	Biggest earnings

How teenagers spend their time in Orange and Maplewood, New Jersey

ACTIVITY	HOURS SPENT WEEKLY
81% WATCH TV	11.3
77.6% LISTEN TO THE RADIO	9.7
47.5% DATING	8.2
83.8% HOMEWORK	9.2
61% TALKING ON THE PHONE	4.4
46.3% DOING NOTHING	8.0

WHEN ARE YOU OLD ENOUGH

to: Wear Make-Up : 13-14

Wear High Heels : 16

Pick Out Your Own Clothes : 13

Go Out With Boys In A Group : 13-14

Start Dating : 15-16

GETTING BELOW THE SURFACE

50% of the young men interviewed in a college survey say that in dating good looks is the least essential characteristic they look for.

spring

When young men's fancies turn to girls' panties

Defying disciplinary action by college officials and police, male students across the nation stage panty and bra raids on women's dormitories.

It must be the PANTY RAIDS

Enrollment in colleges and universities is up for the first time since 1949.

WHAT A YEAR IT WAS!

SCHOOL ROOM CRISIS —  1952

The National Education Association reports that the nation has only one qualified teacher for every five vacancies.

The Fault Lies In The Bureaucracy, Dear Brutus

A survey published in "The New York Times" reveals that of the nation's 3,500,000 elementary and high school students, one out of eight in the public school system is being inadequately educated due to poor facilities.

and they're teaching our kids!!

An embarrassed Los Angeles School Board reports they will correct the misspelling of "language" on the new report cards which is spelled "langauge."

The Merits Of Not Being Educated In L.A.

13-year-old Doris Ann Hall of Hudson, North Carolina wins the National Spelling Bee correctly spelling the word "vignette."

WHATEVER HAPPENED TO "SEE JANE RUN?"

More than half the world's population is illiterate.

FAVORITE CAREERS
STUDENTS AT DENVER'S EAST HIGH SCHOOL

GIRLS	BOYS
Model	FBI Agent
Airline Stewardess	Secret Service Agent
Secretary	Policeman
Homemaker	Cattle Rancher
	Doctor

■ High school and college teachers are now required to teach drug awareness under a new law passed in New York State.

The question is . . . WHY???

The number of foreign students studying in the U.S. hits an all-time high of 30,000.

THE SCORE
(Number of Students Completing Their Education)

ELEMENTARY SCHOOL
7 out of 10

HIGH SCHOOL
1 out of 3

COLLEGE
1 out of 16

POLITICIANS *in the making*

A poll of undergraduates at San Jose State College reveals that more than half the students had cheated on exams and half of them said they would cheat again.

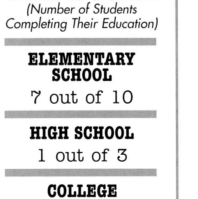

WHAT A YEAR IT WAS!

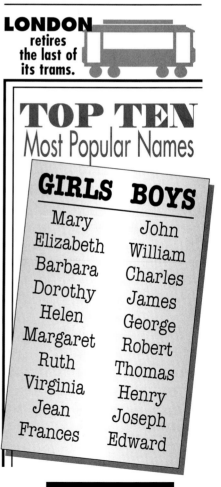

GAS

LODGING

FOOD

Americans spend more money on their cars than any other item except food with yearly expenditures breaking out as follows for the average $2,000 car:

Gasoline, Oil & Repairs	$340
Insurance & Licenses	100
Depreciation	450
Total:	**$890**

AUTO INSURANCE

Insurance company statistics reveal that 80% of all car accidents are caused by 20% of motorists with the worst drivers being between 18 and 25 years of age.

New Jersey introduces **"no fault"** insurance assuring compensation of up to $5,000 whether or not the driver at fault is insured or financially responsible.

PMS x 104 = *WOE* TO BE THE KING

Saudi Arabian King Ibn Saud orders 20 Cadillac limousines to caravan his four wives and 100 ex-wives.

THEY DON'T BUILD THEM LIKE THIS

ANYMORE Traveling 168.4 miles on a single gallon of gas, a rebuilt 1924 Chevrolet wins the annual mileage marathon.

Lots Of Sunday Drivers
Two-thirds of American families own an automobile.

THEY'RE ON THE ROAD AGAIN

According to the American Automobile Association, about half the nation's population took a pleasure trip this year with roughly 85% of them traveling by car.

Over 17 Million People Visit Our National Parks This Year with 96% Arriving By Car.

I say there Old Chap, I think you have the right of way

"More Courtesy" is the theme of Britain's Royal Society for the Prevention of Accidents road safety campaign.

Keep Those Quarters Handy
The new 118-mile New Jersey turnpike is carrying double the traffic forecast and a dozen states are now planning to build new toll superhighways.

The average car lasts 12 years and is good for 100,000 miles.

Trying To Stop The Attack Of The Litterbugs

A reduction in roadside cleanup is attributed to trash bags given to motorists visiting several western national parks with the request that they use them during their stay as well as stickers with the slogan: "Don't Be a Litterbug."

LONDON retires the last of its trams.

TOP TEN
Most Popular Names

GIRLS	BOYS
Mary	John
Elizabeth	William
Barbara	Charles
Dorothy	James
Helen	George
Margaret	Robert
Ruth	Thomas
Virginia	Henry
Jean	Joseph
Frances	Edward

WHAT A YEAR IT WAS!

UP, UP, UP, UP AND AWAY

1952

Piloted by Bill Bridgeman near Edwards AF Base, the Douglas Skyrocket sets a new world record flying 1,238 mph reaching an altitude of 79,494 feet.

FATALITIES ON U.S. AIRLINES FALLS TO THE LOWEST ON RECORD.

Launched at New Mexico's White Sands Air Force Base, the Navy's **Viking 9** breaks the record soaring 135 miles high at a speed at 3,900 mph.

A British Canberra twin-jet bomber becomes the first plane to fly round-trip over the Atlantic in one day, from Aldergrove, Ireland to Gander, Newfoundland and back. It also sets an eastward crossing speed record of 3 hours, 25 minutes.

Refueling in the air, a squadron of **THUNDERJETS** fly from California to Hawaii in a record six hours.

The Sixth Annual Powder Puff Derby is won by **Shirley A. Blocki** and co-pilot **Martha R. Baechle** of Long Beach, California with an average speed of 104.052 mph.

The 1952 Harmon International Aviation Awards:

AVIATRIX JACQUELINE AURIOL
Set a new women's speed record of 532.92 mph breaking her own record of 508.09 mph.

CHARLES F. BLAIR, JR.
The first man to fly a single-engine fighter plane nonstop across the North Pole.

LT. CARL J. SEIBERLICH
For developing new techniques in the use of low-flying planes.

PAN AMERICAN
is first commercial U.S. airline to buy jet planes for passenger use.

DOES THE FARE INCLUDE *pretzels?* 95 passengers land in Shannon, Ireland on TWA's first tourist class flight.

Coffee, Tea or Crumpets?
The world's first jet passenger service commences on British Overseas Airways with a 4 3/4-hour round-trip flight from London to Rome.

A CHILLING EXPERIENCE Alaska Air Command reports U.S. Air Force pilots Lt. Colonel Joseph O. Fletcher and Lt. Colonel William P. Benedict fly first plane to land on the North Pole, a ski-and-wheel equipped C-47.

Parcel post service and helicopter mail begins in New York.
TWO U.S. AIR FORCE **SIKORSKY H-19**'s LAND IN SCOTLAND ON FIRST HELICOPTER FLIGHT OVER ATLANTIC.

A regulation issued by President Truman requires 8,000 conscientious objectors to give two years of national service.

hell no, they didn't go!

The FBI reports it has tracked down nearly 20,000 draft evaders since the passage of the 1948 Selective Service Act.

The Elite Special Forces To Train In Guerrilla Warfare And Counter-Insurgency Is Established By The U.S. Army.

OFFICIALLY TYING THE KNOT

The U.S. Air Force begins using the nautical system of knots and nautical miles replacing "miles per hour."

Published in London, ***Jane's Fighting Ships*** reveals that the U.S. Navy is as large as all the other navies of the world combined.

S.S. United States wins the Blue Riband, crossing the Atlantic from Ambrose Light outside New York harbor to Bishop Rock, Land's End, England in three days, ten hours, 40 minutes breaking **Queen Mary's** record of three days and 20 hours.

WHAT A YEAR IT WAS!

1952

More than 57% of the world's telephones are operating in the U.S.

- Transatlantic telephone service between New York and London hits the 25 year mark.

- Speaker of the House, Sam Rayburn, declares that under House rules committee hearings must ban television, newsreel cameras and tape recorders.

It's 25 years since the first public demonstration of television over telephone wires.

and on the 8th day –
THEY PRINTED

The U.S. Post Office issues a three-cent stamp commemorating the printing of the first book printed from movable type – **The Gutenberg Bible.**

PUBLISHERS POLL
U.S. Newspapers Best Living Up To Journalistic Ideals

N.Y. Times

St. Louis Post-Dispatch

Christian Science Monitor

N.Y. Herald Tribune

The following men's adventure and exposé magazines sell a combined total of 9 million copies at the newsstand:

Adam
Man's Day
Man's Life
Esquire
Fury
Cavalier
Mr. America
Stag
Male
Saga

HONEY

SOMEONE TOOK AWAY THE LAKE
Unable to retrieve their rowboat which had drifted to the middle of the lake, two 14-year-old boys pull the flood gates on artificial Lake Manalapan in Jamesburg, N.J. turning it into a mudflat.

A CHILLING ENDING
Temporary bleachers constructed in a Baltimore armory for the Sonja Henie ice show collapse injuring 275 people.

BRIDGING A FOUR-MILE GAP
The world's third longest bridge is completed on Chesapeake Bay, 25 miles south of Baltimore.

CONSTRUCTION BEGINS ON THE THIRD TUBE FOR THE LINCOLN TUNNEL.

NO JOKING MATTER
With more than 300 titles, comic books continue to be the biggest newsstand grosser.

There's Uranium in them there hills
Hundreds of people begin claim-staking rush at new uranium find in Uranium City, Saskatchewan.

WHAT A YEAR IT WAS!

CHOP CHOP

The most popular lumber types cut:

DOUGLAS FIR	WHITE FIR	COTTONWOOD
PONDEROSA PINE	YELLOW POPLAR	BEECH
OAK	REDWOOD	LARCH
HEMLOCK	SPRUCE	IDAHO WHITE PINE
SOUTHERN PINE	MAPLE	CYPRESS
EASTERN WHITE PINE	TUPELO	BIRCH
RED GUM	CEDAR	LODGEPOLE PINE
	SUGAR PINE	

The three leading lumber producing states are Oregon, California and Washington.

GREEN THUMB EXTRAORDINAIRE

For his outstanding contribution to horticulture, the gold medal of the National Association of Gardeners is awarded to Henry F. du Pont of Wilmington, Delaware.

LEAFING THROUGH

New England is plagued with the rapidly-spreading Dutch elm disease.

Rain Followed By No Rain

Hundreds of customers in 26 states begin receiving scientific weather forecasts thanks to the telegraph company which acts as agent for the weather forecasting services of the National Weather Institute.

Whew! Let's Get Those Hydrants Turned On

New York experiences the hottest calendar month in recorded history as July temperatures average 87.1 degrees.

A HEADY EXPERIENCE

Taking a new route through Nepal, a Swiss expedition of climbers come within 150 ft. of reaching the summit of Mt. Everest, the highest mountain in the world.

SOME CALL ME EVEREST BUT YOU CAN CALL ME CHOMOLUNGMA

Red China announces that henceforth Mt. Everest will be known by the ancient name of Chomolungma, the name Tibetan natives use in referring to the world's highest mountain.

awakening from the long sleep

Dormant for 18 years, Halemaumau, firepit of Kilauea volcano in Hawaii National Park, has a spectacular eruption.

Five consecutive weeks of smog causes $500,000 worth of damage to Southern California crops.

The Bird of Paradise becomes the official flower of Los Angeles.

Boston bans suggestive strip-teasers and female impersonators from nightclubs.

GREETING CARDS and CRAPS

Tuckahoe, New York Mayor Milton A. Gibbons is convicted of conspiracy to set up a dice table in a stationery store.

narcotics

250 Federal Narcotics Agents arrest over 500 drug dealers in nationwide roundup of narcotics dealers.

Let's Lock Up All Those Old Ladies

New York City bans bingo games in churches and other locations where the game is played.

A COP ON EVERY CORNER

Police forces in American cities continue to increase at a greater rate than the population growth.

Residing in Italy, **Charles "Lucky" Luciano** is named as the chief supplier as 23 people are indicted in San Francisco, charged with conspiracy in the sale of heroin nationwide.

The Supreme Court comes down strongly against the forcible use of a stomach pump used on a suspect to get evidence of a narcotics law violation.

PISTOL PACKIN' RABBIT

A Baltimore man is shot in his sleep by his pet rabbit who hopped on the trigger of his .22-caliber rifle.

TAKING HIS BEST SHOT

A Toledo man is charged with assault and battery after firing at his television screen nine times because of poor reception. Missing each time, he then turned the gun on his wife, fired twice, again missing each shot.

BRUSH UP ON THAT CRIMINAL LAW

The American Bar Association predicts an increase in crime.

BUT WILL ARTFUL DODGING END?

A spot check reveals that eight out of ten people obey the first four "**Don't Walk**" signs put up in New York's Times Square.

How much did you say that hammer cost??

The House Judiciary subcommittee calls "shameful" the Justice Department's recovery of only $300,000 of the more than $21 million fraudulently collected from the government by war contractors.

BARRING INDIGESTION

Disgusted with terrible food, bad mail service and delayed paroles, prisoners at Ohio State Penitentiary at Columbus riot, destroying almost $1,000,000 in prison property.

A CROWNING EXPERIENCE

Monsignor Angelo R. Cioffi's public appeal for the return of two diamond-studded crowns stolen from Brooklyn's Regina Pacis shrine bears fruit as the unknown thieves mail back the treasures.

SHOOT-EM UP, STICK-EM UP, BANG-EM UP

The FBI reports a general increase in most crimes during the first half of 1952 with the largest increase being in robberies followed by burglaries, auto thefts and assaults with deadly weapons.

THEY TURNED as WHITE as a SHEET

The U.S. Government invokes the Lindberg law against ten former Ku Klux Klan members for the first time. They are convicted of kidnapping and conspiracy in Wilmington, North Carolina for kidnapping and flogging a white man and woman whom they transported across the state line.

WHAT A YEAR IT WAS!

U.S. CITIZENS CAN NO LONGER TRAVEL TO IRON CURTAIN COUNTRIES WITHOUT PERMISSION FROM THE U.S. GOVERNMENT.

■ *Contempt charges leveled at six defense attorneys during trial of eleven U.S. Communist leaders upheld by the U.S. Supreme Court 5-3.*

■ *U.S. Justice Department announces the arrest of Communist Party leaders in the Midwest and West Coast.*

■ *Fourteen Communist leaders in California are found guilty by a federal jury of conspiring to teach and advocate the overthrow of the U.S. government by force and violence.*

■ *Requiring Oklahoma state employees to take a loyalty oath is declared unconstitutional by the U.S. Supreme Court.*

TWO THUMBS UP

The FBI receives an average of almost 20,000 new fingerprints daily for the identification division's files.

SOVIET PERIODICAL AMERIKA AS WELL AS RUSSIAN INFORMATION BULLETINS ARE BANNED IN THE U.S.

WHAT A YEAR IT WAS!

Eight teachers are dismissed in New York for alleged Communist activities.

Hell No, They Won't Sign

California State Supreme Court rules the University of California's loyalty oath is unconstitutional and the 18 teachers who refused to sign are reinstated.

Guilty until proven Innocent

New York City's Board of Education fires six teachers for refusing to tell a Senate subcommittee whether or not they are members of the Communist Party.

STICKS & STONES
WILL BREAK MY BONES, BUT NAMES WILL NEVER HARM ME

The Brooklyn Supreme Court rules that it is not slanderous to call somebody a Communist.

Thanks, But No Thanks

With its famine relief donation contingent upon the distribution of food being made by a Communist-sponsored committee, the Indian government returns the food to Communist China.

The General Is Seeing Red

Head of the CIA, **General Walter B. Smith**, asserts that Communists have infiltrated almost every U.S. security organization, including the CIA.

Mahn, I Deeg Dis Prayin' Stuff

A musical mass sung in the syncopated rhythm of calypso is offered to the congregation of St. Luke's Church in Cambridge, England.

DO AMERICANS BELIEVE IN GOD?
Catholic Digest Poll

	YES	MAYBE
Roman Catholics	92%	7%
Baptists	93%	6%
Methodists	86%	11%
Lutherans	80%	17%
Presbyterians	90%	8%
Episcopalians	77%	17%
Congregationalists	72%	20%
Jews	70%	18%

Women	100%
Men	98%
High School Grads	99%
College Students	94%

FUNNY, YOU DON'T LOOK 40ish

Girl Scouts of America turn

40

THEIR CLAIM IS GOING UP IN SMOKE

The Federal Trade Commission files suit in New York to prevent Liggett & Meyers from advertising that Chesterfield cigarettes "prevent irritation."

EXTRA

PASSINGS

FDR's beloved Scottish Terrier **Fala** dies just two days before his twelfth birthday.

•

Famed progressive educator **John Dewey** dies at age 92 of pneumonia. Author and philosopher Dewey established a method of learning by doing, which revolutionized American education.

•

World-renowned reformist educator **Dr. Maria Montessori** dies at age 81. Beginning in Italy, her style of open-minded teaching, which became the world-famous Montessori Method preschool system that gave children a more hands-on experience, eventually spread to countries around the world. Montessori toured many nations teaching her method, and she was the first woman to obtain an M.D. from the University of Rome.

•

Commander **Charles Herbert Lightoller**, the only officer to survive the "Titanic," dies at age 78.

•

Catskill icon **Malka Grossinger**, creator of the famed Grossinger's, dies at age 81.

New Words & Expressions

FEDERATED FUND
An organization devoted solely to charity donations.

GROUPMENT
An Armed Forces detachment comprised of 13,000 men.

AIR-WATCHER
A professional who looks to the heavens for suspicious aircraft.

LIKE-IKE
A proponent of presidential-hopeful Dwight D. Eisenhower.

JOB-HOPPING
Changing to a better profession.

PANELIST
One who is part of a panel.

ASTRAGATOR
One who travels between planets.

PANTY RAID
A harmless raid on college girls' dormitories by college boys looking to steal girls' panties.

ATOMIC CALENDAR
An instrument that can determine the age of matter thousands of years old.

PENTAGONESE
Rhetoric used by the Pentagon.

PROFIT FOUL
A deliberate foul.

BAFFLEGAB
The doublespeak and lengthy explanations commonly given by government agencies and workers.

SCIENCER
A science fiction movie.

SHADOW TOWN
A makeshift village for use during combat.

CHOGIE
Name given by American soldiers fighting in Korea to describe an easily identifiable place or thing.

SNIDERY
One who is duplicitous or insincere.

TAXI RADAR
A device that expands the capabilities of airport traffic controllers.

EPISODE PICTURE
Several unconnected tales that make up one film.

STROKELET
A small stroke.

CRASH JOB
Getting a job done quickly.

COSTUMES BY ADRIAN

Setting for Sociability

...that no other travel can match!

On New York Central, there's *room* for sociability. Over refreshments or cards in the lounge car . . . or over a grand, freshly prepared meal, enjoyed at leisure at your dining car table.

There's a sociable atmosphere, too. For you're not gripping a wheel . . . or worrying about the flying weather ahead. You're at ease . . . relaxed . . . with a deep-down sense of security in *any* weather.

Comfort of body. Comfort of mind. You're sure of both on New York Central. And they add up to an overnight vacation that no highway or skyway can equal.

Privacy If You Prefer! Loaf, read or work till bedtime in your own hotel-room-on-wheels. It's a pleasant preparation for a wonderful *Water Level Route* sleep that will get you there tomorrow, rested, refreshed, with energy at peak!

New York Central

The Water Level Route—You Can Sleep

ENTERTAINMENT 1952

MOVIES

Critics call it *"thrilling," "sensational"* and a *"revolution in motion pictures,"* as Hollywood introduces the first Cinerama feature – **This is Cinerama** – screened in New York using a new film projection system with a wide-angle screen, invented by Fred Waller.

LOOK OUT YOU DON'T GET HIT BY A FLYING BWANA

Hollywood debuts **Bwana Devil** starring **Robert Stack** and **Barbara Britton** introducing *Natural Vision*, the second new movie process to be introduced this year. In order to achieve the 3-dimensional effect, the audience wears inexpensive throw-away polaroid glasses.

THE AFRICAN ADVENTURE THAT OUT-THRILLS THEM ALL!

BWANA DEVIL

THRILLING COLOR

starring
ROBERT STACK
BARBARA BRITTON · NIGEL BRUCE

PUT IT IN A HORN 'TILL IT WAS WORN INTO A BLUE NOTE

FRANK SINATRA records **Birth of the Blues** for Columbia Records.

RCA Victor releases a memorable recording of **BEETHOVEN'S Symphony Number Nine** played by the NBC Symphony Orchestra under the direction of **Arturo Toscanini**.

TELEVISION

Premiering the first early-morning television show, **Today**, hosted by **Dave Garroway**, NBC Vice President Pat Weaver predicts it will change the listening habits of America.

Jackie Gleason is dubbed the freshest comedian of the year.

Abbott And Costello Meet Captain Kidd
Anything Can Happen
Apache War Smoke
April In Paris
The Bad And The Beautiful
Battle Zone
Because Of You
Because You're Mine
The Belle Of New York
Bend Of The River
BEWARE, MY LOVELY

The Big Sky
THE BUSHWACKERS
BWANA DEVIL
Clash By Night
Come Back, Little Sheba
THE CRIMSON PIRATE
deadline – u.s.a.
Don't Bother To Knock
Dreamboat
THE FIRST TIME
Flesh And Fury
The Four Poster
The Greatest Show On Earth
The Half-Breed
Has Anybody Seen My Gal?
HIGH NOON
I Dream Of Jeannie
I WANT YOU
THE IMPORTANCE OF BEING EARNEST
IVANHOE
Japanese War Bride
The Jungle
Kansas City Confidential
The Las Vegas Story

70

Les Miserables
LIMELIGHT
MACAO
The Marrying Kind
The Member Of The Wedding
THE MERRY WIDOW
Million Dollar Mermaid
Monkey Business
Moulin Rouge
MY COUSIN RACHEL
MY SIX CONVICTS
PAT AND MIKE
Phone Call From A Stranger
The Pride Of St. Louis
THE PRISONER OF ZENDA
The Quiet Man
Rainbow 'Round My Shoulder
RED PLANET MARS
Road To Bali
Room For One More
Ruby Gentry
The San Francisco Story
SCANDAL SHEET
SCARAMOUCHE
Scarlet Angel
She's Working Her Way Through College

Singin' In The Rain
SKIRTS AHOY!
The Snows Of Kilimanjaro
Somebody Loves Me
Something For The Birds
Something To Live For
SON OF ALI BABA
Son Of Paleface
THE STAR
Stars And Stripes Forever
The Story Of Robin Hood
The Story Of Will Rogers
Sudden Fear
The Thief
THIS IS CINERAMA
The Turning Point
WASHINGTON STORY
WHAT PRICE GLORY
Where's Charley
With A Song In My Heart

1952

Oscar Night IN HOLLYWOOD

Fans assemble to cheer on their favorite stars.

N.J. Bloomberg, President of Universal-International Pictures, and Mrs. Bloomberg, *(below)* lead a parade of celebrities including **JIMMY STEWART,** who graciously signs an autograph, and his lovely wife *(right)*.

WHAT A YEAR IT WAS!

The night is bright with stars. JULIA ADAMS is here with her husband to witness the presentations.

SHELLEY WINTERS and **TTORIO GASSMAN** attend he 24th annual awards *right)* as do MR. & MRS. DONALD O'CONNOR *(below).*

Also attending the festivities is that grand old veteran of the screen, **CHARLES COBURN**, accompanied by his adoring wife *(right).*

It is a year marked by fine films. Beautiful **GREER GARSON** accepts the award for **VIVIEN LEIGH** for her Best Actress performance in *A Streetcar Named Desire.*

Miss Garson presents the Best Actor award to **HUMPHREY BOGART** for his performance in *The African Queen.*

AT A YEAR IT WAS!

The Academy Awards

"And The Winner Is..."

Oscars Presented in 1952

BEST PICTURE
An American In Paris

BEST ACTOR
HUMPHREY BOGART, *The African Queen*

BEST ACTRESS
VIVIEN LEIGH, *A Streetcar Named Desire*

BEST DIRECTOR
GEORGE STEVENS, *A Place In The Sun*

BEST SUPPORTING ACTOR
KARL MALDEN, *A Streetcar Named Desire*

BEST SUPPORTING ACTRESS
KIM HUNTER, *A Streetcar Named Desire*

BEST SONG
"IN THE COOL, COOL, COOL OF THE EVENING," *Here Comes The Groom*

Humphrey Bogart

1952 Favorites (Oscars Presented In 1953)

BEST PICTURE
The Greatest Show On Earth

BEST ACTOR
GARY COOPER, *High Noon*

BEST ACTRESS
SHIRLEY BOOTH, *Come Back, Little Sheba*

BEST DIRECTOR
JOHN FORD, *The Quiet Man*

BEST SUPPORTING ACTOR
ANTHONY QUINN, *Viva Zapata!*

BEST SUPPORTING ACTRESS
GLORIA GRAHAME, *The Bad And The Beautiful*

BEST SONG
"HIGH NOON (DO NOT FORSAKE ME, OH MY DARLIN'," *High Noon*

Gary Cooper

WHAT A YEAR IT WAS!

CAMERA
plus FLASH
plus CASE
only
$69.50

More people buy the <u>Argus C3</u>
than any other 35^M_M Camera!

It sets the pace in *sales* because it sets the pace in *performance*! And this exclusive combination of features tells you why:

A color-corrected, hard-coated f:3.5 Cintar lens gives you sparkling, clear pictures—black and white, or color—even in failing light. A lens-coupled rangefinder gives you sharp, sure focus at any distance from three feet to infinity. A gear-controlled shutter gives you speeds up to 1/300 second for thrilling action shots. Plug-in flash is factory-synchronized . . . no dangling wires, nothing to adjust.

America's favorite way to look at color slides —Argus PBB 200 projector. Triple condensing optical system puts up to 35% more light on the screen. Four-inch lens gives a 32" x 48" true-color image at 12 feet. Silent blower keeps valuable slides cool. Many other exciting features. Complete package—projector, blower and case —an unmatched value at only **$49.50**

argus

—world's largest manufacturer of 35 mm cameras!

World's easiest camera to use—Argus 75! Ask your Argus dealer to show you the attractively priced Argus 75 gift package. You get the Argus 75, leather case, plug-in flash unit, batteries, flash lamps and film. A complete kit for taking wonderful pictures—black and white, or color.

Argus 75 – camera only **$15.95**

All prices include Federal Excise Tax where applicable and are subject to change without notice.

© 1952 Argus Cameras, Inc., Ann Arbor, Michigan

WOMEN'S HOME COMPANION

MOVIE POLL
Most Popular Stars

MALES
Gregory Peck
Clark Gable
Jimmy Stewart

FEMALES
Jane Wyman
June Allyson
Bette Davis

Gable

Davis

NATIONAL BOARD OF REVIEW OF MOTION PICTURES *The Best Of 1952*

The Quiet Man
High Noon
Limelight
Five Fingers
The Snows Of Kilimanjaro
The Thief
The Bad And The Beautiful
Singin' In The Rain
Above And Beyond
My Son John

FOREIGN FILMS

Breaking The Sound Barrier

The Man In The White Suit

Forbidden Games

Beauty And The Devil

Ivory Hunter

🏅 The **N.Y. Film Critics** name *HIGH NOON* the best film of the year.

🏅 *A STREETCAR NAMED DESIRE* is the first film to win three of the four acting Academy Awards.

🏅 *AN AMERICAN IN PARIS* is the third musical to win a Best Picture Academy Award.

🏅 The **Veterans of Foreign Wars** honor comedian **BOB HOPE** with the first Al Jolson Award for entertaining our soldiers at home and abroad.

Hope

🏅 **JOHN WAYNE** is named by **The Motion Picture Herald** as the most popular actor of the year for the second year in a row.

DANCING AROUND TO A DIFFERENT TUNE

At a salary of $15,000 a week, boxing champ **SUGAR RAY ROBINSON** takes over as MC, tap dancer and comic at the French Casino in New York.

Garland

OVER THE TOP OF HER RAINBOW

JUDY GARLAND performs at New York's Palace Theater in a record-breaking engagement.

The Department of Commerce
Average Statistics 1952

Cost of a Hollywood Film: $900,000

Movie Admission: $.47

Refreshments: $.06 (movie theatres)

Refreshments: $.20 (drive-ins)

IS THIS ANY WAY TO COURT A LADY?

A Los Angeles judge issues a warrant for the arrest of JUDY GARLAND after she fails to appear to testify in a lawsuit between her fiancé Sid Luft and his ex-wife Lynn Bari. Judy does show up two hours late thus avoiding jail.

WHAT A YEAR IT WAS!

BIG BUCKS
AT THE BOX OFFICE

Gary Cooper
Bing Crosby
Doris Day
Susan Hayward
Bob Hope
Jerry Lewis & Dean Martin
Gregory Peck
Randolph Scott
Jimmy Stewart
John Wayne

STARS
OF TOMORROW

Marge & Gower Champion
Mitzi Gaynor
Rock Hudson
Kim Hunter
Marilyn Monroe
Audie Murphy
Debbie Reynolds
Danny Thomas
Forrest Tucker
David Wayne

TOP GROSSING SUMMER PICTURES

The Greatest Show On Earth
Jumping Jacks
Tales Of Hoffman

WHAT A YEAR IT WAS!

HOLLYWOOD
Pays Tribute To Its
STARS OF TOMORROW

TYRONE POWER congratulates LORI NELSON and TAB HUNTER who were chosen by film fans throughout the world in *PHOTOPLAY* magazine's annual *"Choose Your Stars Poll."*

Blue-eyed and blond Lori triumphs over the second ranking actress in the poll by a 3-1 margin.

1952

THEY REALLY ARE SOMEBODIES

John Wayne, **Mario Lanza**, **Jimmy Durante**, **Sid Caesar** and **Imogene Coca** make this year's edition of *Who's Who in America*.

Taylor

Elizabeth Taylor announces that she and her husband **Michael Wilding** are expecting a baby.

Roy Rogers' horse **Trigger** sires a son, **Easter**, the day on which he is born.

Quipping that *"A man must be lucky enough to find a patient, gracious lady,"* 71-year-old **Cecil B. DeMille** celebrates his golden wedding anniversary.

After divorcing her fourth husband, **Hedy Lamarr** comments that while love is great, marriage is disappointing.

Audrey Hepburn announces her forthcoming marriage to **James Hansen**, the ceremony to be performed at Huddersfield Parish Church in Yorkshire, England.

FAMOUS BIRTHS

Chazz Palminteri
Christopher Reeve
Dan Aykroyd
Gus Van Sant
Isabella Rossellini
Jeff Goldblum
Liam Neeson
Mary McDonnell
Patrick Swayze
Pierce Brosnan
Roberto Benigni
Robin Williams
Tovah Feldshuh

HOLLYWOOD celebrates its 50th anniversary

In The Making

HENRY FONDA is going to shoot the film version of **Mr. Roberts** next summer.

ROSEMARY ("Come On-a My House") **CLOONEY** is scheduled to make her film debut in **White Christmas** starring **BING CROSBY** and **FRED ASTAIRE**.

HUMPHREY BOGART to star in **STANLEY KRAMER'S The Caine Mutiny**.

Scheduled to make her first film in 20 years, **MARY PICKFORD** drops out of **STANLEY KRAMER'S Circle of Fire** because it is being shot in black and white and not Technicolor.

Broadway's "King" **YUL BRYNNER** is slated to make his movie debut in **A New Kind of Love**.

THE JOURNALIST AND THE PRINCESS
Based on Princess Margaret's adventures in Italy, filming is scheduled to begin in Rome on **Roman Holiday** starring **GREGORY PECK** and **AUDREY HEPBURN**.

Openings

ESTHER WILLIAMS,
Million Dollar Mermaid

MARILYN MONROE,
Don't Bother To Knock

RONALD REAGAN,
The Winning Team

DEAN MARTIN & JERRY LEWIS,
Sailor Beware

WHAT A YEAR IT WAS!

The Danish Foreign Office protests Hollywood's version of the life of **Hans Christian Andersen** starring **Danny Kaye** on the grounds that Andersen is depicted as a man who sang and danced his way through life.

GOD SAVE US FROM SMALL MINDS THAT CAN'T RECOGNIZE BRILLIANCE

Agreeing it *"would tend to corrupt morals"* an Albany, New York Appelate Court upholds a N.Y. State Board of Regents ban on the French movie **La Ronde**.

Called *"morally bad and crime-inciting"* the 37-year-old film classic **Birth of a Nation** is banned by Maryland's Board of Censors.

Rita Hayworth's dance in **Affair in Trinidad** co-starring **Glenn Ford** is deemed too torrid to get past the censors and has to be reshot.

The U.S. Supreme Court reverses both its 1915 judgment and the courts of New York's ban on **The Miracle**, unanimously holding that motion pictures are entitled to the constitutional guarantees of free speech and free press.

WHAT A YEAR IT WAS!

Passings

One of the goofy Three Stooges, **Jerome "Curly" Howard**—ballroom dancer, ukulele player and singer—dies at age 48.

Singer, dancer and actress in the movies and on Broadway, **Dixie Lee Crosby**, who gave up her career after marrying Bing Crosby, dies of cancer three days before her 41st birthday. At the time of their marriage, Dixie Lee was the bigger star and headlines read, *"Dixie Lee marries band singer."*

Fox Film Corp. founder **William Fox**, whose company eventually merged with 20th Century Pictures to become 20th Century Fox, dies of a heart attack at age 73. Fox began in show business by buying a nickelodeon, built up and eventually lost his $300 million company during the Depression and spent a short time in jail for obstructing justice.

First black Academy Award winner for her role of Mammy in "Gone With The Wind," actress **Hattie McDaniel**, star of vaudeville, radio, television and film, dies of cancer at age 57.

New York Lower East Side native **John Garfield**, whose real-life tough guy demeanor translated to the silver screen and Broadway, dies of a heart attack at age 39. As a youngster Garfield learned boxing and acting, and eventually starred in "Body and Soul," "Force of Evil" and "Gentleman's Agreement." Approximately 10,000 fans view his body before burial, an outpouring of emotion not seen for an entertainer since Rudolph Valentino's death.

Garfield

Philip G. Epstein, collaborator on many films with his twin brother including "Casablanca," which won them the Academy Award for Best Screenwriting, dies at age 42.

Billy Graham suggests to producer **David O. Selznick** and actor **Ronald Reagan** that the reason there are so many low-grossing films is that people are sick of sex and crime in movies and suggests they be eliminated so decent people start going to the movies again.

BUT WHAT WILL THEY DO WITH ALL THAT POPCORN?

Samuel Goldwyn predicts that half of the nation's movie theatres will be closed within five years.

Once the mainstay of Hollywood, "B" pictures will be a thing of the past as Warner Bros. and 20th Century Fox announce their discontinuation.

Warner Bros. announces that it is selling control of its 300 movie houses to Fabian Enterprises, making it the third largest movie chain in the U.S.

HE'S BACK

Named to RKO's new board of directors, **Howard Hughes** is back in control of the company after selling his 929,000 shares of stock.

New York Mayor **Vincent Impellitteri** attacks movie and television writers for their depiction of Italian criminals.

The Hollywood AFL Film Council charges that employees of Warner Bros. were forced to make contributions to the Eisenhower-Nixon campaign.

A TAXING PROBLEM

Citing extreme tax burdens, **Cecil B. DeMille** announces the dismantling of his 35-year-old production company.

IS BURBANK BURNING?

Actors **Burt Lancaster, Ray Bolger, Steve Cochran, Gordon MacRae** and studio Vice President **Jack Warner** help save whatever they can as the biggest blaze in Hollywood history destroys over eight acres of Warner Bros. studios including Studio 21, its biggest soundstage.

THE WITCH-HUNT CONTINUES

Despite their denial under oath of any connection to the Communist Party, the Senate Internal Security Subcommittee names **Judy Holliday, Philip Loeb, Sam Levenson** and **Burl Ives** as prominent personalities exploited by the Communists to advance its subversive programs.

A HUNTING WE WILL GO

RKO'S **Howard Hughes** rejects 11 stories out of 150 scheduled for filming on the grounds that the writers are suspected of being Communist sympathizers.

Washington withholds a visa from **Charlie Chaplin** pending investigation into his loyalty.

Much to the chagrin of **Ingrid Bergman**, a Los Angeles judge rules that her 13-year-old daughter Pia Lindstrom must not be compelled to visit her mother in Italy this summer.

AND NO COMMERCIALS, TO BOOT

The Council of Motion Picture Organizations receives reassurances from Hollywood film executive **Dore Schary** that television will never replace movies.

Losing a 14-year legal battle, Loew's Inc., parent company of MGM, agrees to split into two separate divisions—one for production and distribution and one for exhibition.

Corinne Calvet files a $1,00,000 slander suit against **Zsa Zsa Gabor** three days before the release of her latest film, *What Price Glory*.

HEY ABBOTT, CAN YOU GET ME OUT OF THIS MESS?

Comedian **Lou Costello** is arrested for drunk driving and driving without a license.

Walter Pidgeon is elected new president of the Screen Actors Guild succeeding **Ronald Reagan**.

HE LOST HIS FOOTING ON THIS ONE

Gregory Peck suffers several torn ligaments and a ruptured blood vessel in his left knee as he attempts to carry **Ava Gardner** during the shooting of *Snows of Kilimanjaro*.

WHAT A YEAR IT WAS!

TELEVISION

Hey Mom, What's On TV Tonight?

The Adventures Of Ellery Queen
The Adventures Of Superman
The Adventures Of
   Wild Bill Hickok
The Aldrich Family
Amos 'n' Andy
Armstrong Circle Theatre
Arthur Godfrey's Talent Scouts
The Arthur Murray Party
Beat The Clock
Bob And Ray
The Bob Hope Show
Boston Blackie
Break The Bank
Cavalcade Of Stars
Captain Video And His
   Video Rangers
The Dinah Shore Show
Ding Dong School
Double Or Nothing
The Ed Sullivan Show
Ford Theatre
The Frank Sinatra Show
The Fred Waring Show
Gangbusters
The Gene Autry Show
The George Burns And
   Gracie Allen Show
The Goldbergs
I Love Lucy
I've Got A Secret
The Jack Benny Show
The Kate Smith Evening Hour

Kukla, Fran & Ollie
The Lone Ranger
Lux Video Theatre
Meet The Press
Mr. District Attorney
Mr. I Magination
The Original Amateur Hour
Paul Whiteman's Goodyear Revue
The Paul Winchell-
   Jerry Mahoney Show
The Perry Como Show
Philco TV Playhouse
Police Story
The Red Skelton Show
The Roy Rogers Show
The Sammy Kaye Show
The Steve Allen Show
Stop The Music
The Stork Club
The Stu Erwin Show
Studio One
Suspense
Texaco Star Theatre
Tom Corbett, Space Cadet
Twenty Questions
Victory At Sea
What's My Line
Wheel Of Fortune
You Asked For It
You Bet Your Life
Your Hit Parade
Your Show Of Shows

WHERE ARE THE MOST TELEVISION SETS?

1. United States
2. Great Britain
3. Cuba

The Associated Press, *the world's largest news agency, begins a new service, television film news.*

The first Canadian *television broadcast is made from Montreal by the* **Canadian Broadcasting Corp.**

The world's most *powerful television station,* **WSAZ,** *begins telecasting from Huntington, West Virginia.*

WHAT A YEAR IT WAS!

What's New
On The Boob Tube

A Date With Judy
The Adventures Of Ozzie & Harriet
Cavalcade Of America
Chance Of A Lifetime
China Smith
Death Valley Days
The Doctor
Dragnet
The Eddy Arnold Show
Enterprise
The Ernie Kovacs Show
Four Star Playhouse
I Married Joan
I've Got A Secret
The Jackie Gleason Show
Jane Froman's U.S.A. Canteen
Meet Millie
Mr. & Mrs. North
Mr. Peepers
My Friend Irma
My Hero
My Little Margie
Our Miss Brooks
Ramar Of The Jungle
The Range Rider
Rebound
The Red Buttons Show
See It Now
Scott Music Hall
Short Short Dramas
Today
This Is Your Life
Two For The Money
The Walter Winchell Show

Margaret Dumont

Red Buttons

George Reeves

Faces On T.V.

Abbott & Costello
Eddie Albert
Morey Amsterdam
Eve Arden
Jim Backus
Orson Bean
Ralph Bellamy
Joe E. Brown
Billie Burke
Eddie Cantor
Kitty Carlisle
Art Carney
Pat Carroll
Jackie Coogan
Richard Crenna
Walter Cronkite
Dagmar
Don DeFore
Melvyn Douglas
Margaret Dumont
Irene Dunn
Jimmy Durante
Dan Duryea
Ralph Edwards
Dale Evans
Jackie Gleason
Gale Gordon
Reverend Billy Graham
Alan Hale, Jr.
Bob Hope
Artie Johnson
Cloris Leachman

Joe E. Brown

Jack Lemmon
Martin & Lewis
Robert Q. Lewis
June Lockhart
Ida Lupino
Groucho Marx
The McGuire Sisters
Butterfly McQueen
Audrey Meadows
Clayton Moore
Garry Moore
Harry Morgan
David Niven
Donald O'Connor
Jack Paar
Patti Page
Bert Parks
Drew Pearson
Ezio Pinza
Dick Powell
Vincent Price
John Raitt
Tony Randall
George Reeves
Eva Marie Saint
Larry Storch
Gale Storm
Dick Van Patten
Mike Wallace
Ethel Waters
Jack Webb
Marie Wilson

Joe DiMaggio is a little nervous as he makes his TV debut at Yankee Stadium as a baseball commentator.

"Joe DiMaggio's Dugout," a weekly series of televised films about baseball, makes its TV debut.

DiMaggio

The first union contract between actors and television film producers is announced.

The AFL Screen Actors Guild stages a strike against 8l producers of filmed television commercials demanding higher pay and limitations on reruns.

KING OF TELEVISION LOSES HIS CROWN

For the first time since **Milton Berle** went on the air with his *Texaco Star Theatre* in 1948, he loses his No. 1 spot to *Arthur Godrey's Talent Scouts* and as if that's not bad enough, *Arthur Godfrey & His Friends* occupies the No. 2 spot pushing Uncle Miltie to No. 3.

Later in the year, *I Love Lucy* ratings surpass **Arthur Godfrey** and **Milton Berle** putting her show in the #1 spot. It also becomes the first regularly scheduled television program to be seen in ten million American homes.

Our Miss Brooks' Eve Arden

While still a radio success, the first television film of *Our Miss Brooks* airs on CBS.

American Bandstand begins as a local Philadelphia music show.

Singer **Patti Page** makes her television debut as a summer replacement series for **Perry Como**.

MMMMMM WAAAAA
Dinah Shore signs an exclusive television contract with NBC.

Kukla, Fran and Ollie expands from 15 minutes to a half-hour.

Tallulah Bankhead makes her television debut.

The Screen Actors Guild gets producers to agree to additional pay for actors in films that are sold to television.

Seventeen production companies produce 80% of television films.

The FCC authorizes the construction of the nation's first educational television stations.

Jack Gould reports in the "N.Y. Times" on a new method of sending radio signals that could open the way to long-distance television transmission.

MR. POTATO HEAD is the first toy to be advertised on television.

Betty Furness becomes the official **Westinghouse** spokeswoman.

1952

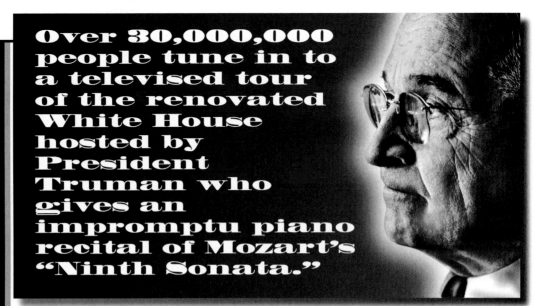

Over 30,000,000 people tune in to a televised tour of the renovated White House hosted by President Truman who gives an impromptu piano recital of Mozart's "Ninth Sonata."

RCA *builds an experimental 5-inch portable TV using an updated application of the transistor.*

•

University of California at Berkeley, *the University of Michigan at Ann Arbor and Western Reserve University are offering courses via video.*

•

The first telecast *from a hospital of a major surgery is seen by television viewers across the country.*

•

The FCC *lifts its freeze on the construction of new television stations.*

WOR-TV announces that it will begin a new type of television programming and will be airing full-length summer stock versions of Broadway plays.

Playwright **Robert E. Sherwood** signs a deal with NBC to write nine original plays.

On a 25-acre lot in Hollywood, CBS dedicates its $12 million Television City.

Yugoslavia announces plans to build its first television station in Belgrade.

15-year-old soap opera, ***Guiding Light***, is the first daytime radio favorite to broadcast simultaneously on radio and television.

SNIP SNIP

A new position, that of censor, has been created at the TV networks. Duties include cutting scenes from old movies that could be considered objectionable.

Walter Cronkite hosts a series of political telecasts.

- - - - - -

NBC-TV premieres **Victory at Sea,** the first documentary film series to receive wide acceptance.

Cronkite

WHAT A YEAR IT WAS!

"I knew we should have brought that TV set in last!"

SIMPLIFIED, SINGLE-CONTROL TUNING.
Remarkable Target Tuner perfectly synchronizes picture and sound. Filtered-Clear pictures edge to edge with no fade, no drift, no further adjustments.

NEW! ACOUSTINATOR TONE CONTROL
—provides fully variable tone range, from treble to bass, for the famous "Golden Voice" sound—assures you of perfect listening enjoyment.

For television enjoyment

the Picture tells the story©

Smart television shoppers *compare the picture performance* first—and check the ease of tuning, sound, cabinet styling.

That's why smart shoppers pick new 1952 Motorola TV—the *picture tells the story* about finest quality ... at lowest prices.

MOTOROLA TV illustrated, 17 inch Mahogany plastic table model, 17T7.

NO GLARE ANNOYANCE. *Exclusive* Glare Guard eliminates up to 98% of reflected glare. Optically curved screen and non-reflecting Absorbalite tube direct outside light interference down and away from the screen, out of eye range ... for greater viewing comfort.

© 1952, MOTOROLA INC.,   *Specifications subject to change without notice.*

EXCLUSIVE NEW AREA SELECTOR SWITCH—3-position switch boosts power for "fringe" reception ... new Concentrated Power Chassis has revolutionary simplified circuits. improved compact design. You're assured of finer, more dependable reception in town or 'way out-of-town!

For the picture of the year, it's the buy of the year

19 Beautiful Models
to choose from ...
as low as $199.95

Motorola TV

proved most dependable

1952

Miss TV

19-year-old Phillis Maygers of Baltimore is named Miss U.S. Television of 1952.

EMMY awards

SERIES

Situation Comedy	**I LOVE LUCY**
Variety	**YOUR SHOW OF SHOWS**
Mystery, Action or Adventure	**DRAGNET**
Audience Participation, Quiz, or Panel	**WHAT'S MY LINE?**
Children's	**TIME FOR BEANY**

PERFORMERS

Comedian	**JIMMY DURANTE**
Comedienne	**LUCILLE BALL**
Personality	**BISHOP FULTON J. SHEEN**

Famous Births

Angela Cartwright

Annie Potts

Carol Kane

Cheryl Ladd

Harry Anderson

Jay North

John Goodman

John Tesh

Laraine Newman

Lou Ferrigno

Mr. T

Roseanne

Susan Dey

WHAT GOES UP, MUST COME DOWN

A congressional committee investigating ethics in television programming notes that the big improvement the industry has made is the raising of ladies' necklines but deplores the proliferation of violent crime shows as well as beer and wine ads.

With television sex and violence growing, 80 out of 108 stations have agreed to comply with a new voluntary code to censor shows that sympathize with evil, degrades virtuous behavior, ridicules authority or fails to punish lawbreakers.

The House Un-American Activities Committee calls Hollywood Communism's biggest financial angel and warns the television industry to guard against Red infiltration.

WHAT A YEAR IT WAS!

1952

TOP TEN
RADIO PROGRAMS
(Evening)

Dragnet	Romance
Railroad Hour	The Gene Autry Show
FBI In Peace And War	People Are Funny
You Bet Your Life	Great Gildersleeve
Life With Luigi	Johnny Dollar

TOP TEN
RADIO PROGRAMS
(Daytime)

Romance Of Helen Trent	Pepper Young's Family
Right To Happiness	Road Of Life
Our Gal Sunday	Big Sister
Ma Perkins	Guiding Light
Backstage Wife	Aunt Jenny

THE END
OF OLD FAVORITES

The Adventures Of Ozzie And Harriet

Big Sister

Big Show

Big Town

Double Or Nothing

The Green Hornet

I Love A Mystery

Inner Sanctum Mysteries *

The Mysterious Traveler

* After an 11-year run with its slowly creaking door and a scary *"Good night,"* this most popular mystery program ends.

CBS Radio celebrates its **25th** anniversary.

WHAT A YEAR IT WAS!

FAMOUS BIRTH Robin Quivers

1952

THE VOICES OF FREEDOM SPEAK

- U.S. and West Germany sign an agreement permitting U.S. broadcasting stations in Munich which will transmit **Voice of America**.

- **Voice of America** launches the **Courier**, the first seagoing radio broadcasting station.

- Radio Free Europe begins operating a new transmitter to beam broadcasts to Poland.

ARCHIE & VERONICA— *MORALLY CORRUPT?*

Moscow Radio accuses America of flooding western Europe with ideological and moral poison in the form of American comic books that corrupt the younger generations in France, Britain and other European countries.

RADIO PROGRAM WITH CLASS

The world's largest radio transcription service, Towers of London, Ltd., sells three new radio series for broadcast in America—**The Scarlet Pimpernel**, **Capt. Horatio Hornblower** and an **Alec Guinness** series.

 **T.V.'s** *My Little Margie* starring **Gale Storm** and **Charles Farrell** makes its radio debut on CBS.

Amos 'n' Andy celebrates its 25th year on the air.

Dick Clark goes to work for WFIL Radio in Philadelphia and begins hosting *Caravan of Music*.

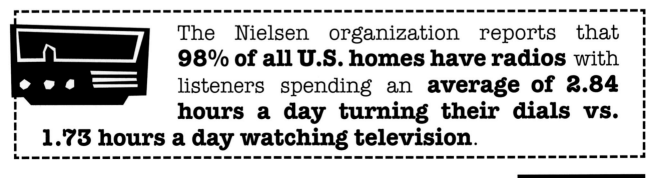

The Nielsen organization reports that **98% of all U.S. homes have radios** with listeners spending an **average of 2.84 hours a day turning their dials vs. 1.73 hours a day watching television**.

POPULAR MUSIC

1952 The HITS

A Full Time Job .... *Eddy Arnold*

A Guy Is A Guy .... *Doris Day*

Anytime .... *Eddie Fisher*

Are You Teasing Me .... *Carl Smith*

Auf Wiedersehn Sweetheart .. *Vera Lynn*

Back Street Affair .... *Webb Pierce*

Be Anything .... *Eddy Howard*

Be My Life's Companion .... *The Mills Brothers*

Because You're Mine .... *Mario Lanza*

Blacksmith Blues .... *Ella Mae Morse*

Blue Tango .... *Leroy Anderson*

Botch-A-Me .... *Rosemary Clooney*

Cry .... *Johnnie Ray*

Delicado .... *Percy Faith*

Don't Let The Stars
   Get In Your Eyes .... *Perry Como*

Easy On The Eyes .... *Eddy Arnold*

Give Me More, More, More .. *Lefty Frizzell*

Glow Worm .... *The Mills Brothers*

Half As Much .... *Rosemary Clooney*

Have Mercy Baby .... *Dominoes*

Here In My Heart .... *Al Martino*

High Noon .... *Frankie Laine*

I Saw Mommy
   Kissing Santa Claus ...... *Jimmy Boyd*

I Went To Your Wedding .... *Patti Page*

I'm Yours .... *Don Cornell*

I'll Walk Alone .... *Don Cornell*

It Wasn't God Who Made
   Honky Tonk Angels ...... *Kitty Wells*

It's In The Book .... *Johnny Standley*

Jambalaya .... *Hank Williams* with
                          his *Drifting Cowboys*

Kiss Of Fire .... *Georgia Gibbs*

Lawdy Miss Clawdy .... *Lloyd Price*

Meet Mr. Callaghan .... *Les Paul*

The Most Beautiful Girl
   In The World .... *Frank Sinatra*

One Mint Julep .... *Clovers*

Pittsburgh, Pennsylvania .... *Guy Mitchell*

Please, Mr. Sun .... *Johnnie Ray*

Rock Around The Clock .... *Sunny Dae*

Takes Two To Tango .... *Pearl Bailey*

Tell Me Why .... *Four Aces*

That Heart Belongs To Me ... *Webb Pierce*

Too Old To Cut The Mustard . *Rosemary Clooney
                          & Marlene Dietrich*

Walkin' My Baby Back Home . *Johnnie Ray*

Wheel Of Fortune .... *Kay Starr*

Why Don't You Believe Me .. *Joni James*

The Wild Side Of Life ..... *Hank Thompson*

Wish You Were Here .... *Eddie Fisher*

You Belong To Me .... *Jo Stafford*

Hank Williams, Doris Day, Eddie Fisher

89

NEW RECORDING ARTISTS ON THE MUSIC SCENE

Four Lads

Bill Haley & His Comets

Joni James

Steve Lawrence

Al Martino

Lloyd Price

MUSIC TO SHOP BY

Background music becomes increasingly popular in supermarkets and other retail stores.

SAM PHILLIPS launches SUN Records

Pfc. Vita Farinola (24), a.k.a. crooner **Vic Damone**, *returns home after serving a year in the U.S. Army and cuts a record called* **The Girls Are Marching** *which the Defense Department will use to recruit 80,000 women.*

Harry Belafonte

records his first songs for RCA Victor at New York's Manhattan Center.

12-year-old **Jimmy Boyd's** *recording of* **I Saw Mommy Kissing Santa Claus** *sells a record 700,000 copies in ten days and hits the #1 spot on the charts.*

Ray Charles SIGNS WITH ATLANTIC RECORDS.

BECAUSE OF HIM THERE'S A SMILE IN THEIR HEARTS

25-year-old crooner **Tony Bennett** *becomes the latest idol of the bobby-sox set at New York's Paramount Theatre.*

The **Swiss National Yodel Festival** *is held in the small city of St. Gall where 2,800 yodelers show up for the competition.*

Famous Births

David BYRNE

Dee Dee RAMONE

George STRAIT

Grace JONES

Joey RAMONE

Lee RITENOUR

Phoebe SNOW

WHAT A YEAR IT WAS!

Better See Motorola Radios

NEW Pin-up Clock Radio

in four decorator colors

Model 52CW $39⁹⁵*
Slightly higher
South and West

"Timer Too!"

time the eggs . . . or it switches on your favorite program when you want it

Here's a new idea—it's Motorola Pin-Up Clock Radio, designed for every one of you who has ever said, "Give me a clock I can see clear across the room . . . and a radio that doesn't take up shelf space!"

But that's not all, Motorola added a magic timer that turns on your favorite radio program automatically!

Wonderful for kitchen, bathroom, rumpus room, den, and porch, and in your choice of four decorator colors—cherry, leaf, off-white, citron. Notice the attractive design, the clock face made for easy reading, the smooth bakelite finish that wipes clean in a split-second. Then turn the dial and listen to the *Golden Voice* of radio with its big-set tone. See it—hear it now—it's a wonderful idea for putting your minutes to music all around the house!

Kitchen: Choose cherry, off-white, leaf, or citron . . . save precious shelf space—use it to time your cooking.

Bathroom: Music while you time your home permanent—a clock to help get you dressed in time for appointments.

Den or Rumpus Room: Use it anywhere — comes complete with wall hooks that make installation a matter of seconds.

Porch: Pin-up music on any wall—and patented outlet plug adjusts cord to exact length to wall socket.

Motorola All-Around the House

as low as
$17⁹⁵*
Slightly higher
South and West
*Prices subject to change without notice

Model 52X in Walnut, Ivory and Maroon.

Model 62C in Walnut, Ivory and Forest Green.

Model 62X in Walnut, Ivory and Forest Green.

Model 52R in Walnut, Ivory, Maroon, Grey, Red and Forest Green.

Motorola *the Golden Voice of Radio*

World's largest exclusive electronics manufacturer

© 1952, MOTOROLA, INC.

1952

All That Jazz

West Coast jazzman, 31-year-old DAVE BRUBECK, impresses the New York jazz scene with his brand new style.

Piano men **Meade Lux Lewis**, **Pete Johnson**, **Erroll Garner** and **Art Tatum** wow the audience at Birdland, Manhattan's mecca of cool.

Woody Herman forms a band including bassist **Chubby Jackson**.

Mercury Records releases JIVE AT FIVE featuring **Count Basie**.

Fletcher Henderson

BIG MAMA THORNTON
makes the first recording of *Hound Dog*.

After scoring successes in Hollywood and London, beautiful black singer **Dorothy Dandridge** sells out Manhattan's La Vie en Rose.

Dorothy Dandridge

Eartha **Kitt** makes her nightclub debut at the Blue Angel in New York.

Jazz musician, composer and band leader **Fletcher Henderson** *dies at age 55. In the early '20's Henderson hired a little-known trumpeter named Louis Armstrong, and at one time worked with Ethel Waters.*

Benny Goodman, the King of Swing, reunites the Benny Goodman Trio—**Gene Krupa** and **Teddy Williams** and ailing **Fletcher Henderson**—for the first time in 13 years to record a new LP for Columbia Records.

SOMEWHERE THERE'S MUSIC

LES PAUL designs the first eight-track tape recorder which is introduced by Ampex.

Gibson releases the **LES PAUL MODEL** solid-body electric guitar.

WHAT A YEAR IT WAS!

RCA VICTOR — *the pick of the portables!*

Easy to take

This handsome portable "45" phonograph is less than one foot square, plugs into any AC outlet, plays up to fourteen 45 rpm records. "Golden Throat" tone system. Maroon plastic case with carrying handle. "Victrola" 45 Personal phonograph, 45EY3, $39.95

Power-plus in handsome blue portable radio. 3-gang condenser for extra-sharp tuning and greater range. AC, DC, or self-contained battery. The "Globe Trotter" Standard, PX600, $39.50

Plenty of "get-up-and-go" in this good-looking portable! Good listening, too—the tone system is the glorious "Golden Throat." In strong but lightweight alligator grain plastic. Plays on AC, DC, or battery. The "Reveler," BX57, $34.00

Just two inches thick—no bigger than an average book—this trim little portable radio weighs less than 3½ lbs., equipped with a built-in aerial, wonderful tone, plenty of pep and power. The "Personal," B411, $27.50

"Tune in" perfect weather with an RCA Room Air Conditioner.

Prices shown are suggested list prices, less batteries, subject to change without notice and to Government Price Ceiling Regulations. Slightly higher in far West and South.

Remember. RCA Batteries are radio-engineered for extra listening hours. Make sure you get 'em!

RCA VICTOR

Tmks.® DIVISION OF RADIO CORPORATION OF AMERICA

"HIS MASTER'S VOICE"

World Leader in Radio . . . First in Recorded Music . . . First in Television

Classical Music

NEW WORKS

Symphony Concertante
Gail Kubik
(Pulitzer Prize)

Symphony No. 4
Paul Creston

Piano Concerto
Alexei Haieff

Symphony No. 7
Roy Harris

The Temptation of St. Anthony
Gardner Read

Stravinsky

In Los Angeles, **Igor Stravinsky** conducts the first performance of his *Cantata* for solo voices, female chorus and string quintet.

The Edinburgh festival opens with Sir Thomas Beecham conducting a Sibelius program.

Arturo Toscanini's hospital benefit sets advance box office sales record of $64,000.

The Boston Symphony makes its first European tour.

The Danish State Orchestra visits the U.S. for a series of 38 concerts.

Pittsburgh holds its first International Contemporary Music festival which includes programs of symphonic, choral and chamber music by modern composers.

Anderson

Contralto **Marian Anderson** slated to do a repeat performance of her famous 1939 Lincoln Memorial concert in honor of the late Harold L. Ickes.

250 white people in Miami demand refunds when they find out the audience will be not segregated at a **Marian Anderson** concert.

Ending their ban on black artists, the DAR brings in **Dorothy Maynor** making her the first black to sing commercially in the DAR's Constitution Hall in D.C.

THE SOUND HAS A BIG BANG

In Tennessee, The Oak Ridge Symphony Orchestra premieres **Overture to the Dedication of a Nuclear Reactor**, the first serious musical composition inspired by atomic energy, written by Arthur Roberts, associate professor of physics at the University of Rochester.

A PIPING HOT SCOOP

The Vice Director of the Bagpipe Players College of Glasgow sadly admits that the famous Scottish highland bagpipes originally came from Cremona, Italy where in 1515 a Scottish tourist first heard the bagpipes and brought them back to Scotland.

WHAT A YEAR IT WAS!

Opera News

New Operas

Leonard Bernstein conducts his first one-act opera, *Trouble in Tahiti*, at a festival of the creative arts at Brandeis University in Waltham, Massachusetts.

Arthur Kreutz's *Acres of Sky* debuts in New York City.

The Farmer and the Fairy by **Alexandre Tcherepnin** premieres in Aspen, Colorado.

Hans Werner Henze writes *Boulevard Solitude*.

A new Swiss opera, *Leonore 40/45* written by **Rolf Liebermann**, has its premiere.

Bluebeard's Castle by **Bela Bartok** and **Bela Balasz** receives its first staging by New York City Opera.

British composer **Benjamin Britten** is commissioned to compose a coronation opera based on the affairs of Elizabeth I and the Earl of Essex.

George and Ira Gershwin's opera **Porgy and Bess**, starring **Leontyne Price**, **Cab Calloway** and **William Warfield**, is sent to Europe under State Department auspices and receives ovations in Vienna and Berlin.

WHAT A YEAR IT WAS!

ENDING ON A LOW NOTE

Metropolitan Opera stars and newlyweds, **Robert Merrill** and **Roberta Peters** sing *Sweethearts* on a New York TV show and five days later they separate citing incompatibility.

Kicked out of the Metropolitan Opera by **Rudolph Bing** for leaving before the end of the season, baritone **Robert Merrill** sends a letter of apology and asks that he be taken back, which Bing agrees to.

With ticket prices scaled as high as $7.20, 70,000 paying patrons fill theatres in 27 cities to see Richard Tucker starring in *Carmen*, the first live performance of an opera beamed via closed-circuit television directly from the Metropolitan Opera.

The Met opens its 68th season with a new production of **Verdi's** *La Forza del Destino*

Composer **Gian-Carlo Menotti** scores raves for an evening of his music at Manhattan's Lewisohn Stadium including excerpts from his operas *Amelia Goes to the Ball*, *The Consul*, *Amahl and the Night Visitors*, *The Island God*, *The Old Maid and the Thief* as well as segments of his ballet *Sebastian* and his *Piano Concerto*.

With masks designed by **Jean Cocteau** who also wrote the libretto, composer **Igor Stravinsky** conducts his opera *Oedipus Rex* in Paris.

The Love of Danae, the only unperformed opera by **Richard Strauss**, premieres at the Salzburg Festival.

Mezzo soprano **Rise Stevens** performs *Carmen* at the Met and her performance is called *"sensational."*

Alban Berg's opera *Wozzeck*, with **Dimitri Mitropoulos** conducting, is performed at La Scala for the first time and is well received.

Robert Merrill

Roberta Peters

Maria Callas

At La Scala 30-year-old MARIA CALLAS receives bravos for her performance in Mozart's *Abduction from the Seraglio*.

Dance

Ballet Theatre

ALONSO • YOUSKEVITCH KRIZA • MOYLAN and the French stars BABILEE and PHILIPPART

Program: "Constantia" "Circo de Espana", "Til Eulenspiegel" "Theme & Variations".

BROOKLYN ACADEMY OF MUSIC

Lafayette Ave. & Ashland Pl. 1 Block off Subs. Tickets: $1.20, $1.80, $2.40, $3, $3.60. Box Off Now. ST 3-6700. Also McBride's, B'way at 43d at Regular Prices.

The Bali dancers along with their orchestra of Balinese percussion instruments are flown to the U.S. under the auspices of the cultural department of Indonesia.

The newly-organized **Mia Slavenska-Frederic Franklin Ballet** makes its New York debut with the premiere of a choreographed version of **Tennessee Williams'** *A Streetcar Named Desire*.

Henri Sauguet's *Cordelia* and **Georges Auric's** *Coup de feu* make their debuts at the Paris ballet festival.

The **New York City Ballet** performs *Age of Anxiety* at the 1952 International Exposition of the Arts.

Agnes de Mille's new ballet, *The Harvest According*, is given its world premiere by the **Ballet Theatre** at the Metropolitan Opera House in New York.

After being abroad for five months touring London, Paris, Florence, Edinburgh, Holland, Belgium, Switzerland and Spain, the **New York City Ballet** winds up its tour at the Berlin Festival.

The fifth American Dance Festival is held at New London, Connecticut where new works premiere including *The Queen's Epicedium*, music by **Henry Purcell**, and *The Visitation*, music by **Arnold Schoenberg**, both choreographed by **Jose Limon**.

The **Sadler's Wells Theatre Ballet** makes its New York City debut.

At the ripe old age of 34 **Jerome Robbins**, who joined George Balanchine's New York City Ballet in 1948, decides to stop dancing.

Maria Tallchief is one of five ballerinas dancing in George Balanchine's new ballet, *Caracole*.

Hanya Holm's dance script for *Kiss Me Kate* becomes the first dance script to be accepted by the register of copyrights of the Library of Congress.

Margot Fonteyn receives an honorary Doctor of Letters degree from Leeds University.

Ben Sommers receives The American Fashion Critics award for his adaptation of ballet slippers for offstage wear.

The BBC broadcasts square dance music as square dancing gains new popularity both in America and abroad.

Arthur Murray names **Alfred Hitchcock, The Duke of Windsor, Vivien Leigh, Bernard Gimbel** and **Zsa Zsa Gabor** as some of the best nonprofessional dancers of the year.

WHAT A YEAR IT WAS!

ON BROADWAY

CRITICS CALL THIS BROADWAY SEASON THE POOREST SINCE THE TURN OF THE CENTURY.

EARTHA KITT GETS A HOT REVIEW FROM BROOKS ATKINSON OF THE NEW YORK TIMES FOR HER OUTSTANDING PERFORMANCE IN "NEW FACES OF 1952."

1952

ANOTHER OPENING, ANOTHER NIGHT

Beatrice Grayson and **John Garfield** in *Golden Boy*

E.G. Marshall, Arthur Kennedy and **Beatrice Straight** in *The Crucible*

An Evening With
Beatrice Lillie

❋

The Children's
Hour (revival)

❋

The Climate
Of Eden

❋

The Crucible

❋

Electra (revival)

❋

First Lady (revival)

❋

Golden Boy (revival)

❋

The Grass Harp

❋

In Any Language

The Male Animal

❋

Mrs. McThing

❋

The Millionairess

❋

Of Thee I Sing
(revival)

❋

The Seven Year
Itch

❋

Time Of The Cuckoo

❋

Time Out
For Ginger

❋

Venus Observed

❋

The Victim

❋

Wish You
Were Here

98

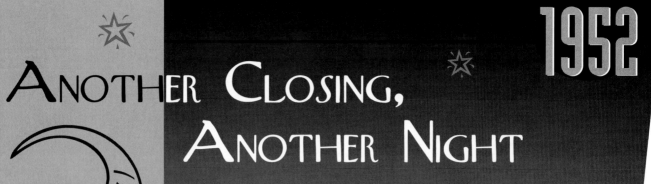

ANOTHER CLOSING, ANOTHER NIGHT

Bagels & Yox

☆

Call Me Madam

☆

Gigi

☆

I Am A Camera

☆

The Millionairess

☆

Paint Your Wagon

☆

The Shrike

☆

The Victim

Audrey Hepburn and **Cathleen Nesbitt** in *Gigi*

WHAT A YEAR IT WAS!

Tony Awards
1952

PLAY
"The Fourposter"
Jan de Hartog (playwright)

MUSICAL
"The King And I"
Oscar Hammerstein II (book/lyrics)
Richard Rodgers (music)

DRAMATIC ACTOR
Jose Ferrer
"The Shrike"

DRAMATIC ACTRESS
Julie Harris
"I Am A Camera"

DIRECTOR
Jose Ferrer
"The Shrike," "The Fourposter,"
"Stalag 17"

MUSICAL ACTOR
Phil Silvers
"Top Banana"

MUSICAL ACTRESS
Gertrude Lawrence
"The King And I"

NEW YORK DRAMA CRITICS' CIRCLE AWARD

BEST AMERICAN PLAY	**I AM A CAMERA**
BEST FOREIGN PLAY	**VENUS OBSERVED**
BEST MUSICAL	**PAL JOEY** (revival)

SPECIAL AWARDS

JUDY GARLAND for her performance at the Palace Theater.

CHARLES BOYER for "Don Juan in Hell."

Pulitzer Prize for Drama
The Shrike
Joseph Kramm

HOT Off The Presses

Hemlock and After
(Angus Wilson)

Winter Journey
(Clifford Odets)

Waiting for Godot
(Samuel Beckett)

The Silver Chalice
(Thomas B. Costain)

DID YOU HEAR THE ONE ABOUT THE GUY WHO KILLS THE KING AND THEN HIS WIFE GOES CRAZY (YUK YUK)

Tired of the same old Shakespeare year after year, residents of Stratford-upon-Avon, old Bill's birthplace, vote to spend over $500 a week for vaudeville shows.

Famous Birth | **Mandy Patinkin**

BROADWAY'S TOP TEN

SOUTH PACIFIC
GUYS AND DOLLS
THE MOON IS BLUE
THE KING AND I
THE FOURPOSTER
POINT OF NO RETURN
PAL JOEY
THE MALE ANIMAL
NEW FACES OF 1952
WISH YOU WERE HERE

The *Mousetrap* by **Agatha Christie**, starring **Richard Attenborough** and his wife, **Sheila Sim**, opens at the Ambassadors Theatre in London.

Charles Laughton, Agnes Moorehead, Charles Boyer and **Sir Cedric Hardwick** give a reading of **Bernard Shaw's** new play, *Don Juan In Hell.*

Katharine Hepburn sails to London on the liner "America" to star in Shaw's *The Millionairess.*

Hepburn

The opening in Stockholm's Royal Dramatic Theater of *The Living Room*, the first play written by novelist **Graham Greene,** is twenty minutes late as the author is stuck in an elevator.

Bette Davis is slated to star on Broadway in *Two's Company,* her first musical comedy.

HERE'S SINGING TO YOU, KID

Ezio Pinza and **Marlene Dietrich** offered the Bogart/Bergman roles in a Broadway musical version of *Casablanca.*

NO MORE WAITING FOR LEFTY

Elia Kazan says he was a member of the Communist Party for only two years and left in disagreement along with playwright **Clifford Odets.**

IS YOU IS OR IS YOU AIN'T A COMMIE

Prolific playwright **Lillian Hellman** denies being a Communist but won't say whether or not she ever was.

A new contract with Broadway producers calls for a minimum salary for actors of $85 a week in New York and $110 on the road.

Washington's National Theatre reopens on a nonsegregated basis with a four-week run of *Call Me Madam.*

Since American actors don't get hired very often in England, Actors Equity announces restrictions on alien actors from seeking employment in the U.S.

PASSING

British actress **Gertrude Lawrence**, theatre star on both sides of the Atlantic, was starring on Broadway as Anna in "The King & I" at the time of her death at age 54. Lawrence entertained troops during World War II, and childhood friend Noel Coward wrote "Private Lives" for her.

Bud Collyer and Roxanne, Stars of "Beat The Clock"

To be sure of Outstanding Performance say SYLVANIA!

Watch that Sylvania Picture Tube! You'll see scenes so vivid and bright you might think you could reach out and touch them.

Why this amazing performance? You'll find the answers in Sylvania's leadership in those specialized fields that make picture tubes possible, namely *radio, electronics,* and *lighting.* These also are the reasons why 75% of today's top TV set makers use Sylvania Picture Tubes. Make sure your set is equipped with one!

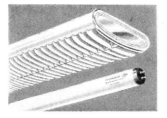

Fluorescent Tubes and Fixtures. Sylvania Fluorescent Fixtures fit any interior. Sylvania Fluorescent Tubes, with improved coil coatings and fluorescent powders, *guarantee* more light, for a longer time.

Light Bulbs. Sylvania Light Bulbs are made to highest standards of efficiency and long life. At every manufacturing step, they're tested to make good their slogan: "The Best Light in Sight."

Photoflash Bulbs. For perfectly detailed photos, use Sylvania Superflash* Bulbs. The famous Blue Dot and Quick-Flash filament make every shot a *sure shot.* Remember—*"Blue Dots for Sure Shots."*

*Sylvania trade-mark

Radio and Television Sets. Sylvania TV sets now bring you "HaloLight"*... a soft border of light that frames your TV picture, reduces contrast ... makes pictures seem larger, more realistic.

Don't miss "BEAT THE CLOCK" Sylvania's hilarious TV show ... every week over CBS-TV

SYLVANIA

Sylvania Electric Products Inc. ⬧S⬧ 1740 Broadway, New York 19, N.Y.

Hear Sammy Kaye's SYLVANIA SUNDAY SERENADE Sunday Afternoons, ABC Radio Stations

RADIO TUBES; TELEVISION PICTURE TUBES; ELECTRONIC PRODUCTS; ELECTRONIC TEST EQUIPMENT; FLUORESCENT TUBES, FIXTURES, SIGN TUBING, WIRING DEVICES; LIGHT BULBS; PHOTOLAMPS; TELEVISION SETS

ART

At The MUSEUM

Many never-before-seen paintings including Non-Objective and Impressionist styles make up a **KANDINSKY** exhibit put on by Boston's Institute of Contemporary Art. The exhibit travels to San Francisco, New York, Minneapolis and Cleveland.

Over 90 pieces by **RODIN** are featured in *"Sculpture of the Twentieth Century"* at the Philadelphia Museum of Art.

A record high of nearly 3 1/2 million people visit the Smithsonian.

The Metropolitan Museum of Art and the Art Institute of Chicago mount the most comprehensive **CEZANNE** exhibit ever shown. 100 pieces are borrowed from museums and individuals on several continents.

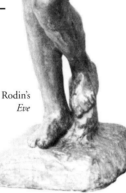

Rodin's
Eve

The 500th anniversary of the great **Leonardo da Vinci's** birth is celebrated around the world with notable exhibits in London, New York, Paris, Los Angeles and his home-town of Florence.

THE NEW YORK ART WORLD

UNIVERSITY OF OHIO PROFESSOR **ROY LICHTENSTEIN** HAS A NEW YORK SHOW.

A **JACKSON POLLOCK** SHOW IN NEW YORK FEATURES 14 NEW PAINTINGS.

TEN~YEAR~OLD TURKISH ARTIST **HASAN KAPTAN** HAS AN EXHIBIT OF HIS BRIGHTLY COLORED PAINTINGS AT A MANHATTAN GALLERY.

JOHN D. ROCKEFELLER, JR. GIVES $10 MILLION TO THE CLOISTERS, PART OF MANHATTAN'S METROPOLITAN MUSEUM OF ART.

FERNAND LEGER MURALS ADORN THE AUDITORIUM OF THE NEW UNITED NATIONS BUILDING IN NEW YORK.

WHAT A YEAR IT WAS!

Surrealist of the century Salvador Dali uses familiar themes such as Tristan and Isolde to make jewel-encrusted jewelry.

Women in Art

Georgia O'Keeffe receives a Litt.D from Mills College.

Georgia O'Keeffe

Francoise Gilot, famed common-law wife of Pablo Picasso, has her first one-woman show at a Paris gallery.

Impressionist **Berthe Morisot** is given a major retrospective at the Toronto Art Gallery. Morisot's daughter lends 30 paintings only after the museum agrees to insure them for approximately $1 million.

History is made as women become trustees of the Metropolitan Museum of Art for the first time. **Mrs. Vincent Astor** and **Mrs. Ogden Reid** are two of the trend setting ladies.

Presidential candidate **Dwight D. Eisenhower** *is the first actual person to be on the cover of the* SATURDAY EVENING POST. **Norman Rockwell** *is the artist.*

The only remaining **Michelangelo**, "Rondanini Pieta," to remain in private hands is sold to the city of Milan for $216,000.

A little painting stored in an attic in Scotland thought to be nothing worthwhile turns out to be **Pieter Bruegel's** "Christ and the Woman Taken in Adultery" from 1565 and sells for $31,000 at a London auction.

ACQUISITIONS

DELACROIX	*Turkish Women in the Bath*
	Wadsworth Atheneum, Hartford, CT
EL GRECO	*Portrait of a Trinitarian Monk*
	Nelson Gallery, Kansas City, MO
PICASSO	*Night Fishing at Antibes*
	Museum of Modern Art, NY
DE KOONING	*Excavation*
	Art Institute of Chicago, IL
RENOIR	*The Washerwoman* (sculpture)
	Philadelphia Museum of Art, PA
RUBENS	*The Tiger Hunt*
	Wadsworth Atheneum, Hartford, CT

Over 300 paintings from two dozen countries are exhibited at the **39TH ANNUAL CARNEGIE INTERNATIONAL.**

A few well-known names exhibited at the **26TH VENICE BIENNALE:**

UNITED STATES	Edward Hopper	FRANCE	Fernand Leger
	Alexander Calder (winner of the President's Prize for sculpture)		Henri de Toulouse-Lautrec
			Raoul Dufy (winner of the President's Prize)
ENGLAND	Graham Sutherland		
SPAIN	Francisco de Goya		

Edward Hopper's etching *Evening Wind*

WHAT A YEAR IT WAS!

oui oui

For an extensive exhibit, German museums lend Paris' l'Orangerie 80 Impressionist paintings by **Renoir, Van Gogh, Sisley, Pissarro, Cezanne, Courbet, Corot** and **Manet**.

Two teenage art lovers break into Paris' Museum of Modern Art and are caught red-handed cutting several masterpieces from their frames. The damaged paintings – a **Bonnard** ("Self-Portrait"), a **Gauguin** ("Ia Orana Maria"), a **Renoir** ("Seated Nude") and a **Picasso** ("Woman Ironing") – are on loan from America.

Impressionist paintings collected by the late **DR. GACHET** are donated to the Louvre by his children. The paintings, done by many of his friends including **RENOIR, MONET, VAN GOGH** and **PISSARRO**, have never been viewed in a museum. Also donated are palettes and other objects used by the artists.

Dr. Gachet by Van Gogh

WHAT A YEAR IT WAS!

ON THE PARIS AUCTION BLOCK

CEZANNE
"Apples and Biscuits"

$110,031
highest price ever paid for a Cezanne

RENOIR
"Young Girl with Flowers in Her Hat"

$75,021

VAN GOGH
"The Thistles"

$55,015

Parisians flock to the Galerie Royale for "The Art Gallery of the Future," a show that uses lights and pre-recorded, taped explanations to highlight specific works of art.

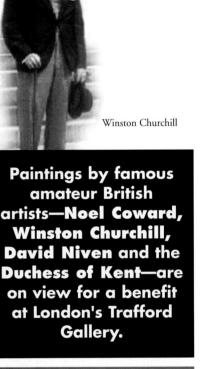
Winston Churchill

Paintings by famous amateur British artists—**Noel Coward, Winston Churchill, David Niven** and the **Duchess of Kent**—are on view for a benefit at London's Trafford Gallery.

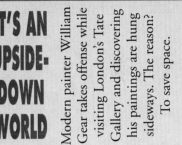

IT'S AN UPSIDE-DOWN WORLD Modern painter William Gear takes offense while visiting London's Tate Gallery and discovering his paintings are hung sideways. The reason? To save space.

NEWS FROM LOS ANGELES

The Los Angeles City Council reverses last year's ruling that modern art is a *"tool of the Kremlin."* Meanwhile, a Republican Representative from Michigan accuses Artists' Equity Association of being a Communist front.

In Los Angeles, "Paintings from the George Gershwin Collection" features works by **Soutine, Chagall, Utrillo,** playwright **Clifford Odets** and **Gershwin's** own "Portrait of Arnold Schoenberg."

Here's proof you can own a genuine **Bigelow** *for less than* $160

You won't believe it till you see the price tags! But your Bigelow dealer has a wide and wonderful selection of exquisite carpets priced on the budget side of $160. Gorgeous patterns . . . textures . . . tone-on-tones! All the wonderful styles you love in luxury carpets.

Today Bigelow brings you these fabulous carpets at modest prices. For Bigelow's exciting new carpet yarns and improved weaving techniques have succeeded in lowering the cost of high style.

See these thrilling new carpets at your Bigelow dealer's today. Whether you spend under or over $160 . . . be the proud owner of a genuine Bigelow.

Cordalon†—a blend of wool and Bigelow's special carpet-rayon. Beautiful with contemporary or period furnishings. Choose from 8 luscious colors. About $10.95* a sq. yd.

New Fervak—a luxurious blend of wool and special carpet-rayon yarns. Resists soil, foot- and scuff-marks. Perfect for any room in your house. About $8.50* a sq. yd.

Marimba—winner of the Home Fashions Award. Beautiful, luxurious, easy to keep clean. Available in 7 color combinations. 100% carpet-rayon. Only about $8.95* a sq. yd.

Quality-tested to bring you years of satisfaction. Bigelow Carpets are subject to many rigid tests—equivalent to years of average home use.

Would you ever guess this handsome 9'x12' carpet costs about $157.00.* It's Bigelow's BEAUVAIS. All wool, available in modern and traditional patterns. A wonderful value in room sizes or wall-to-wall. About $11.95* a sq. yd.

Important! Bigelow carefully selects a limited number of retailers in each community. If you are not *sure* of the name of a local Bigelow retailer, call Western Union by number, ask Operator 25.

Get your copy of "Carpets—Their Selection and Care." 24 pages of helpful, important information. Send your name and address with 10¢ to Home Service Bureau, 140 Madison Ave., N. Y. 16, N. Y.

*Prices subject to change without notice and slightly higher in the West.
†Reg. U. S. Pat. Off.

Bigelow *rugs and carpets*

Beauty you can see *. . . quality you can* trust *. . . since 1825*

ARCHITECTURE + DESIGN

The citizens of Florence take to the streets and protest new skyscrapers being built that go against the centuries-old traditional feel of the town.

●

The new United Nations building in Manhattan is estimated to be worth $33 per square foot.

World-famous founder of the ßauhaus style, Walter Gropius resigns after 15 years at Harvard's Graduate School of Design.

Frank Lloyd Wright is elected to the American Academy of Arts and Letters. He also receives the City of Florence's Gold Medal and has an exhibit in Paris entitled "Sixty Years of Living Architecture."

Le Corbusier's latest apartment complex opens in Marseille, France.

A model of R. Buckminster Fuller's dome-shaped Geodesic House is on view at New York's Museum of Modern Art.

oogie? no, googie!

Los Angeles' Googie makes national news. The whimsical, organic, modern style is best seen at Googie's Sunset Boulevard restaurant, where stucco and steel make for a progressive delight.

Style GOOGIE

Regulation X is eradicated by the Federal Reserve Board and the Housing and Home Finance Agency, eliminating a minimum down payment on new homes.

Following the success of Levittown, New York, the tract housing community of Levittown, Pennsylvania is finished, and 3,000 homes sell within two months.

The country's first mass developed housing complex with air-conditioning is built in Dallas, Texas. The low-cost homes are available for $12,500.

It's one thing to move to another city, it's another to have to find a residence you like as much as your old one. The new Unishelter movable house solves this dilemma. It can be taken apart and put back together in a matter of hours, so relocating becomes as simple as packing.

FURNITURE

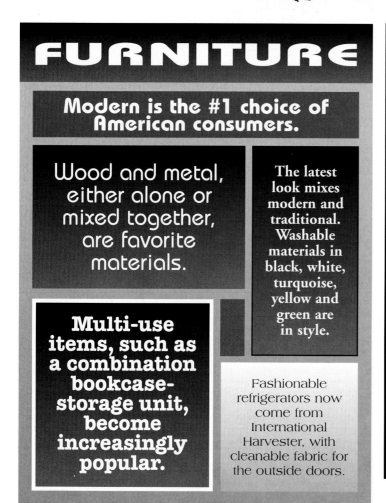

Modern is the #1 choice of American consumers.

Wood and metal, either alone or mixed together, are favorite materials.

The latest look mixes modern and traditional. Washable materials in black, white, turquoise, yellow and green are in style.

Multi-use items, such as a combination bookcase-storage unit, become increasingly popular.

Fashionable refrigerators now come from International Harvester, with cleanable fabric for the outside doors.

GOODBYE, FDR

Elliott Roosevelt sells his father's beloved home and 500 acres of property in Hyde Park, New York for roughly $150,000.

Jewels by Harry Winston

A *Great Experience* Awaits You!

We sometimes think that a motorist never *fully* appreciates his Cadillac until he has owned and driven it for a goodly time. To be sure, his very first ride introduces him to comfort, performance and pride of ownership that he has never experienced before. But there are *many* wonderful things about a Cadillac which only the years and the miles can reveal. There is, for instance, the car's extraordinary dependability. There is its astonishing economy—so marvelous that a full day's journey can usually be made on a single tankful of gasoline. And there is its all but unbelievable endurance —so great that there is no practical limit to the car's life and utility. We thought you'd appreciate knowing, as you look forward to your first Cadillac, that these wonderful things are true. For it means there's a *great experience* ahead for you— when you make the move to the Car of Cars.

CADILLAC MOTOR CAR DIVISION ★ GENERAL MOTORS CORPORATION

Books

A Many-Splendored Thing
Han Suyin

A Stone For Danny Fisher
Harold Robbins

American Capitalism
John Kenneth Galbraith

Amy Vanderbilt's Complete Book
Of Etiquette

Arrow In The Blue
Arthur Koestler

Be Happier, Be Healthier
Gayelord Hauser

Beyond The High Himalayas
William O. Douglas

The Bicycle Rider In Beverly Hills
William Saroyan

The Build-Up
William Carlos Williams

Casino Royale
Ian Fleming

Charlotte's Web
E.B. White

Chicago: The Second City
A.J. Liebling

The Complete Poems And Plays
T.S. Eliot

Curious George Rides A Bike
H.A. Rey

Dance To The Piper
Agnes de Mille

The Devils Of Loudun
Aldous Huxley

East Of Eden
John Steinbeck

Ethics In Government
Paul H. Douglas

Every Dog Should Have A Man
Corey Ford

The Far Country
Nevil Shute

From Under My Hat
Hedda Hopper

Giant
Edna Ferber

The Glitter And The Gold
Consuelo Vanderbilt Balsan

Grandma Moses:
My Life's History

The Groves Of Academe
Mary McCarthy

Hemlock And After
Angus Wilson

The Hidden Flower
Pearl S. Buck

Homage To Catalonia
George Orwell (posthumously)

How To Succeed In Business
Without Really Trying
Shepherd Mead

I Go Pogo
Walt Kelly

In Country Sleep, And
Other Poems
Dylan Thomas

Invisible Man
Ralph Ellison

The Judgment Of Paris
Gore Vidal

Kiss Me, Deadly
Mickey Spillane

Let It Come Down
Paul Bowles

Lieutenant Hornblower
C.S. Forester

The Lost Childhood
And Other Essays
Graham Greene

PRIZES

NOBEL

Literature

FRANCOIS MAURIAC, FRANCE

PULITZER

Public Service

St. Louis Post-Dispatch

National Reporting

ANTHONY LEVIERIO
New York Times

Local Reporting

GEORGE DE CARVALHO
San Francisco Chronicle

Editorial Writing

LOUIS LACOSS
Saint Louis Globe Democrat

Editorial Cartooning

FRED L. PACKER
New York Mirror

Photography

JOHN ROBINSON & DON ULTANG
**Des Moines Register
and Tribune**

Fiction

HERMAN WOUK
"The Caine Mutiny"

History

OSCAR HANDLIN
"The Uprooted"

Poetry

MARIANNE MOORE
"Collected Poems"

WHAT A YEAR IT WAS!

FAMOUS BIRTHS

Amy Tan

•

Douglas Adams

PASSINGS

Philosopher, author, poet and Harvard professor **George Santayana** *dies in an Italian convent at age 88. Author of* "The Life of Reason," *Santayana came to America as a youngster, never drove a car and never used a typewriter. Said Santayana,* "Those who cannot remember the past are condemned to repeat it."

•

Publisher **David Smart**, *who introduced* "Esquire" *and* "Coronet" *to receptive audiences, dies at age 60.*

Mary Poppins In The Park
P.L. Travers

Men At Arms
Evelyn Waugh

Midcentury Journey
William L. Shirer

Morality In American Politics
George A. Graham

Mrs. Reynolds And Five Earlier Novelettes
Gertrude Stein (posthumously)

My Cousin Rachel
Daphne du Maurier

The Natural
Bernard Malamud

People Of The Deer
Farley Mowat

Player Piano
Kurt Vonnegut, Jr.

The Power Of Positive Thinking
Norman Vincent Peale

Prisoner Of Grace
Joyce Cary

Rage Of The Soul
Vincent Sheean

Revised Standard Version Of The Holy Bible

Secret Tibet
Fosco Maraini

Shiloh
Shelby Foote

The Silver Chalice
Thomas B. Costain

Soft Voice Of The Serpent
Nadine Gordimer

Spark Of Life
Erich Maria Remarque

Spartacus
Howard Fast

The Sundowners
Jon Cleary

Tallulah: My Autobiography
Tallulah Bankhead

This Crooked Way
Elizabeth Spencer

This Was The Old Chief's Country
Doris Lessing

The Thurber Album
James Thurber

The Trouble With Cinderella
Artie Shaw

U.S.A. Confidential
Jack Lait & Lee Mortimer

Wandering Star
Shalom Aleichem

Wise Blood
Flannery O'Connor

Year In, Year Out
A.A. Milne

AMERICAN ACADEMY OF ARTS AND LETTERS

Gold Medal History and Biography
Carl Sandburg

Gold Medal—Fiction
Thornton Wilder

NATIONAL BOOK AWARDS

Fiction
"From Here To Eternity"
James Jones

Nonfiction
"The Sea Around Us"
Rachel L. Carson

1952

MAD MAGAZINE

hits the newsstands.

40 countries sign the General Universal Copyright Convention, protecting writers' rights.

Glamorous as the writing profession may seem, over half of Authors Guild members make under $3,000 yearly.

According to a poll of the nation's youngest book lovers, the tops in kiddie literature are **Cinderella**, **Big Book of Real Fire Engines**, **Jack and the Beanstalk** and **Little Red Riding Hood**.

The Gutenberg Bible is 500 years old.

WHY DON'T YOU COME OVER THE BORDER AND READ ME SOME TIME?

Canada bans over 500 books from being brought into the country, including **Mae West's "Diamond Lil."**

Published several years ago, **"Anne Frank: The Diary of a Young Girl"** is translated into English.

BETTER LATE THAN NEVER

A hundred years after its initial publishing, **Harriet Beecher Stowe's "Uncle Tom's Cabin"** is available in Budapest.

A 20-page section of **Ernest Hemingway's "The Old Man and the Sea"** is printed in "Life" magazine several weeks before the book is released.

TO BUY OR NOT TO BUY, THAT IS THE QUESTION

$1 million is the price paid for a 73-volume collection of **Shakespeare works, notably quartos and folios.**

The British Museum buys **Lewis Carroll's fabled "Alice's Adventures in Wonderland."** The rare first edition is bought from the Duke of Gloucester for close to **$4,000**.

William Shawn becomes editor of THE NEW YORKER.

Special guest **Eleanor Roosevelt** speaks at the American Library Association's yearly conference.

At 2,864 pages, **Madison Cooper's "Sironia, Texas"** is the longest novel ever printed in the United States.

FASHION
Paris

25-year-old Givenchy presents his first couture collection which includes faux animal prints on silk, berets, big flat purses and chunky bracelets.

The house of Dior shows form-fitting black dresses and evening dresses with wide skirts.

Popular materials include pleated chiffon, tweed and lace.

Waists are placed anywhere from the chest to the hip.

Daytime skirts and dresses are slightly longer this year and vary from roughly 11″ to 14″ from the ground. Formal long dresses measure 3″ from the ground.

DESIGNER ELSA SCHIAPARELLI COMPLAINS THAT DESIGNERS, HERSELF INCLUDED, HAVE FORGOTTEN TO MAKE CLOTHES THAT FIT WELL WITH WOMANLY ATTRIBUTES SUCH AS BREASTS AND HIPS, AND HAVE INSTEAD FOCUSED ON THIN, MODEL~TYPE FIGURES.

WHAT A YEAR IT WAS!

1952

SUITS
are more loosely constructed than previous seasons, especially around the waist. Spencer jackets over full skirts are a definite hit.

The shirtwaist dress
has a **form-fitting bodice**, wide skirt and is available in various patterns and colors.

Glamorous **Gloria Swanson**, well guarded, arrives at the Waldorf-Astoria Hotel wearing the world's most expensive gown.

The dress is covered with 100,000 pearls, is worth $100,000 and weighs 30 pounds. It took 15 years to gather the prewar cultured pearls, and eight dressmakers worked two years to complete the job.

The beautiful stage and screen star wears the proper accessories including a pearl necklace with matching ring and stickpin.

The Imperial Pearl Syndicate is donating the gown to the Damon Runyon Fund for cancer research.

This fabulous costume will be shown at a series of benefits throughout the country.

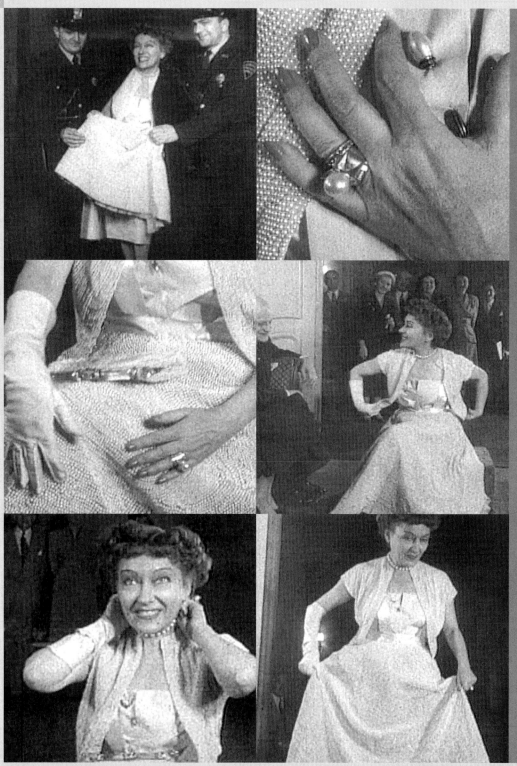

Gloria Swanson turns to fashion designing, and her low-priced line of dresses is available for under $20.

1952

Double seams eliminate the need for stiff boning in undergarments.

Stockings are sheerer than ever before. The average American woman wears a size 10.

According to fashion industry insiders, the best measurements for a woman's leg are 19 1/2″ at the thigh and 8 1/2″ at the ankle.

1952 ADVERTISEMENT

Ring-A-Round by BESTFORM

shaped to serve your curves

the circular stitched bra with a young natural look

Two-needle circular stitched for complete support...a lovely lilting lift...beautiful separation. Styled for easy comfort with a tailored band bottom that can't cut—can't bind—stays just where you want it. A cup, sizes 32-36; B cup, sizes 32-40; C cup, sizes 34-42.

In broadcloth, white only .. **$1.50**
In nylon, white and black .. **$2.00**

BESTFORM

no finer fit at any price

Sold at leading department stores and specialty shops throughout the country

Sewing Tip—
DON'T GET MARRIED

Single gals spend approximately 5 1/2 hours a week at their sewing machines while their married counterparts sew for 8 hours.

Nighttime shopping gains in popularity, and it's estimated that people purchase up to 25% more in the evening hours.

116

WHAT A YEAR IT WAS!

ACETATE STAYS CRISP AND FRESH. Acetate fibers have a natural resiliency that helps fabrics shed wrinkles, keeps you fresh looking all day through, cuts pressing to a minimum.

ACETATE IS SOFT AND LUXURIOUS. Fabrics of acetate are wonderfully soft...feel delightfully comfortable next to your skin. There's no worry about soiling, either—acetate garments come back from the dry-cleaner just about like new.

ACETATE IS EASY TO CARE FOR. A fast sudsing, a quick rinse, hang for a few minutes, and your still-damp acetate garment is ready for the *light, cool* press that is the correct easy way to iron acetate.

Acetate . . . the Fiber That Gives You the Fashions You Love to Wear

Do you know *why* so many beautiful clothes are made of Acetate the Beauty Fiber? It's because acetate makes fabrics that are pretty yet practical—that drape beautifully, yet are easy to care for. No other fiber contributes so many of the things you want in the clothes you wear—as acetate!

WHAT IS ACETATE? Acetate is the man-made textile fiber, cellulose acetate, pioneered by Celanese Corporation of America. Acetate has a unique combination of characteristics that make fabrics wonderfully soft and comfortable. You will find acetate fabrics in all kinds of beautiful suits, lingerie, sportswear, dresses and evening gowns.

ACETATE FABRICS—

Look lovely—feel wonderful

Drape gracefully

Help wrinkle recovery

Launder easily—dry quickly

Dry-clean perfectly

WRITE FOR FREE BOOKLET ON "ACETATE, THE BEAUTY FIBER"

NEXT TIME YOU SHOP LOOK FOR THE TAG . . .

Celanese CORPORATION OF AMERICA • 180 MADISON AVENUE, NEW YORK 16, N. Y.

117

YOUNGSTERS FASHION SHOW

Critical eyes watch approvingly from the sidelines.

All the latest models are on parade during the exhibition of junior creations for the young miss and the young master.

WHAT A YEAR IT WAS!

In Copenhagen

Note that it's not always fair weather that you must prepare for.

Formal attire for the girl and boy of your dreams.

Every wardrobe must include a cowpoke outfit.

And speaking of dreams it's time to say good night.

1952

SOME ENCHANTED EVENING. . .

The short evening dress rises to 10" from the floor, looks best in red, black or pink, and is covered by a cardigan or stole. White evening dresses are improved with embroidery or beads. Large bows add an extra feminine touch.

OUI Y'All

The South of France turns Southern as the latest in Texas-wear is displayed.

Hans Gehringer's clothing designs come to America—the first time a German designer has accomplished this since before the war.

Italian designers continue to gain recognition in America where prices are often half of their more famous French counterparts.

MAMMA MIA

Fashionable maternity clothes from Italy, heavy on elastic and concealed pouches, keep the pregnant woman well put together.

The Queen of England is a style-setter, and her newest dress to catch the world afire is **the magpie**. Worn to a command film performance, the black and white gown is copied and sold off the rack to those with less-than-queenly incomes.

*W*ide, built-in waistbands called *fascias* add texture and drama to dresses day or night and are flattering to the figure. Fascias are also another name for super wide belts, and are available in all kinds of materials.

WHAT A YEAR IT WAS!

COLORS

GREEN is the color of the year, alone or in combination with another hue, often **BLUE**. Other surefire colors include **CAMEL**, **BEIGE**, PURPLE, **YELLOW**, RED and the eternally chic GREY, WHITE and BLACK.

FABRICS & SUCH

POODLE CLOTH IS ONE OF THE TRENDY COAT FABRICS.

Alpaca
Boucle
Crepe
Denim
Embroidery
Faille
Gabardine
Herringbone
Irish Tweed
Jersey
Kidskin
Lamé
Moiré
Nylon
Orlon
Pique
Quill
Roman Silk
Satin
Taffeta
Urban Chic
Velveteen
Wool
eXcellence
Yoke
Zibeline

WHAT A YEAR IT WAS!

You Heel, You

1952

*T*he Oxford and Moccasin are some of the comfiest shoes around.

*H*eel choices include pointy, narrow, stiletto, wedge, Flamenco, curved, square, Louis and spindle.

*R*ed shoes are worn with all colors.

*O*pera pumps, mulebacks and sandals are a must for all female feet.

*R*ibbons & bows are favorite shoe decorations.

The sweater girl look is back in vogue.

Sleeveless sweaters with long sleeved cardigans worn over them are one of the stylish sweater set combos.

College girls are ready for finals and more in sweater dresses, over-blouses, slacks and suits. Their male counterparts wear slim trousers, blazers and mufflers.

GET THEE A HAT!

The finishing touch of any outfit whether a **boater, bonnet, beret, calot, sailor, pillbox, cloche, toque** *or* **striped straw.**

1952 ADVERTISEMENT

**ALL-WOOL PASTEL CHECK
$26 FULL-SWEEP COATS**

19.95

Velvet under-collar, velvet cuffs!
Jewel buttons, Earl-Glo lining.
Costly hand details. Sizes 10-18.
Other coats from 14.95 to 32.95

**MISSES' & WOMEN'S
10.95 SPRING DRESSES**

7.89

Checked rayon menswear and
sheen gabardine; or linen-like
rayon. Sizes 12 to 20; 14½ to 24½.
Other dresses from 3.89 to 14.89

**$25 ALL-WOOL TOPPERS
IN SOFT SUEDES & CHECKS**

18.95

Flattering roll collar. New push-
up sleeves. Earl-Glo rayon satin
lined. Pastels. Sizes 10 to 18.
Other toppers from 7.95 to 23.95

**2-PC. SHEEN GABARDINE
$9 BOLERO SUITS**

6.89

Button-trim bolero, 2-pocket skirt,
medallion belt. Rayon sheen gabardine. Sizes 12 to 18.
$3 Misses' & Women's Blouses 1.89

**GIRLS' SOLID & CHECK
$13 GABARDINE COATS**

8.95

Solid navy with check trim or
check with navy trim. Fine rayon
sheen gabardine. Sizes 7 to 14.
Other coats from 10.95 to 14.95

*NOW buy your clothing the way you buy your
groceries...the super-market low overhead way!*

- Low Rents
- No Costly Show Windows
- No Fancy Fixtures
- Plain Pipe Racks
- Mass Distribution
- No Charge Accounts

**WATER-REPELLENT
$11 GABARDINE JACKETS**

Rayon gabardine. Fully
lined. Sizes 34 to 46. **7.95**
8.50 Rayon Gabardine Slacks 4.95

**BOYS' HARD-FINISH
$18 GABARDINE SUITS**

Crease-resistant rayon
gabardine. 6 to 16. **13.95**
Other suits from 14.95 to 19.95

**$40 "PARADER" SUITS
in FINE SPRING FABRICS**

29.95

Exclusive custom designed patterns. Sharkskins, all-wool flan-
nels, donegal tweeds, coverts.
Other suits from 24.95 to 42.95

**LUXURIOUS ALL-WOOL
$38 SPRING TOPCOATS**

27.95

Venetian coverts, sheen gabar-
dines, Donegal tweeds, checks.
Raglan or set-in sleeves. 34 to 48.
Other topcoats 22.95 to 39.95

**PURE VIRGIN WOOL
$30 SPRING SPORT COATS**

21.95

Superbly tailored 2-button model.
All-wool checks, plaids, herring-
bones, diagonals. Sizes 35 to 46.
$14 Worsted Gabardine Slacks 9.95

ROBERT HALL

COAST
TO
COAST

123

All That Glitters Is

Gold, be it fake, flecked or the costly stuff from the finest stores around, is an accent appropriate on everything:

Gilded bracelets.

Gold & beads, gold & pearls.

Gold lamé evening bags.

Golden-hued gloves.

Glitter on handbags, gloves, shoes, scarves and dresses.

Gold sequined eye shadow.

Golden hair streaks brush on and easily wash out in the shower.

Gigantic gilt pins.

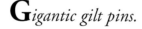

Rhinestones remain a favorite choice for all occasions on large earrings, necklaces, pins or ornamentation on purses and shoes.

124

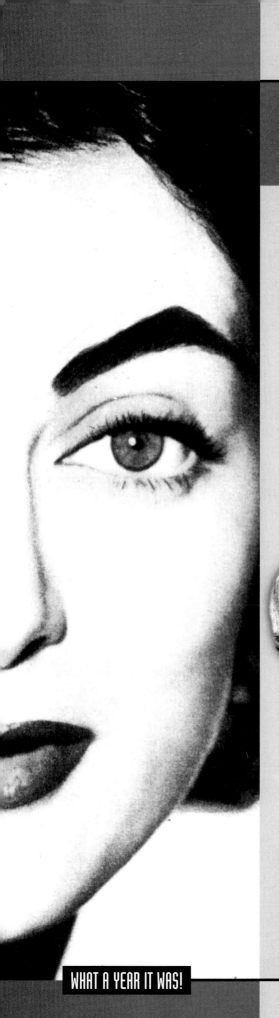

FACE IT!

Eyebrows *are thick and have an accentuated arch.*

Pink *is the prevalent color for lips.*

Sequins *can be placed over lipstick and eye shadow.*

False eyelashes *and black eye shadow add drama.*

Hair *is short, often with waves or put up in a chignon.*

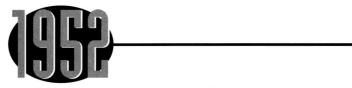

1952

The *Best-Dressed* Group

Women

Ann Sheridan
Barbara "Babe" Paley
Dorothy Kilgallen
Duchess of Kent
Duchess of Windsor (#1 for 10 years)
Jo Stafford
Mamie Eisenhower
Marlene Dietrich
Mrs. Estes Kefauver
Mrs. William Randolph Hearst, Jr.
Vivian Blaine

Men

Arthur Murray
Bernard Baruch
Conrad Hilton
Douglas Fairbanks, Jr.
Ed Herlihy
Gene Kelly
Guy Lombardo
Hank Greenberg
Phil Rizzuto
Robert Alda
Tommy Dorsey
Tyrone Power
W. Averell Harriman

Dietrich

Power

Two chimps at a St. Louis Zoo are given tennis shoes to keep warm in the winter.

500 MILLION PAIRS OF SHOES ARE MADE IN THE U.S.

Famous Birth

Jean-Paul Gaultier

FASHIONS *for* HIM

TALK ABOUT THE FASHION POLICE

In Poland, men who have taken to wearing U.S.A.-style ties have them snipped off in public by officers.

WHAT A YEAR IT WAS!

The snap-brim hat that is worn by fashionable men everywhere.

The raincoat is shorter than previous seasons, reaching almost to the knees.

For a night out on the town wear a pleated white tuxedo shirt, gloves, gold cuff links and a cummerbund.

The au courant suit is single-breasted, brown, and made of rayon, acetate or Dacron. A waistcoat adds color and a finishing touch.

A new combination cotton-Orlon suit is machine washable and drip dries in several hours without any wrinkles.

ARE YOU MAN ENOUGH FOR POWDER?

The Fashion Foundation of America suggests men carry around powder to help eliminate that pesky five o'clock shadow.

Wrinkle-resistant "disciplined" cotton keeps you looking sharp in the city on a humid summer day as well as on the golf course all year 'round.

A bullet-proof nylon vest is being tested in Korea by U.S. infantrymen.

1952 ADVERTISEMENT

You like it ... it likes you !

"fresh up" with Seven-Up!

As full of lively fun as a dimpled drum majorette—sparkling, crystal-clear
7-Up leads the way to thirst-quenching enjoyment. *So pure, so good, so wholesome*
—folks of *all ages* can "fresh up" often with the All-Family Drink!

Copyright 1952 by The Seven-Up Company

Buy it by the CASE or in the
new and handy
7-UP FAMILY PACK →
of 24 bottles!

Easy-lift center handle!   Space saving!   Family supply!

128

New PRODUCTS And INVENTIONS

Driving With A FIFTH WHEEL

New cars are getting bigger and parking spaces are getting smaller.

So, an inventor in Piedmont, California has developed something to soothe the motorist's headache. The spare tire is put to work by activating a switch.

And if you have a narrow driveway, the car can turn a complete circle in its own radius making parking very simple. Even the worst driver can make the garage without denting a fender with the aid of fifth wheel driving.

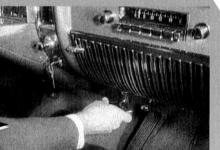

This "fifth wheel driving" device can be installed on any model and here's how it works. Taking power from the drive shaft, the spare tire swings the rear end into the clear.

Then he just retracts the spare, backs into the street and away he goes.

129

1952 ADVERTISEMENT

America's Favorite and Finest Enamel !

Kem-Glo is so practical for bathroom walls . . . withstands steam, moisture.

Kem-Glo keeps woodwork beautiful . . . resists scuffing, is easy to keep clean.

Color-styled from the Color Album, with KEM-GLO in Arbor Green for walls and cabinets, Light Chartreuse for ceiling, Norwood Green for door and Carnival Pink for counter tops . . . all so easy to keep sparkling clean.

**READY-TO-USE...
JUST STIR AND APPLY**

$1⁴⁵ PINT
$2⁴⁹ QUART
$8³⁵ GALLON

The Miracle Lustre Enamel for Kitchens Bathrooms and Finest Woodwork

KEM GLO

Looks and Washes Like Baked Enamel!

Guaranteed by Good Housekeeping

Ask to see the Color Album.
Hundreds of color schemes.

Kem Products Distributed by . . .
Acme Quality Paints, Inc., Detroit
W. W. Lawrence & Co., Pittsburgh
The Lowe Brothers Co., Dayton
John Lucas & Co., Inc., Philadelphia
The Martin-Senour Co., Chicago
Rogers Paint Products, Inc., Detroit
The Sherwin-Williams Co., Cleveland

If you wish, we will gladly recommend a painting contractor for any of your painting needs.

The DeLuxe Wall Paint

SUPER Kem-Tone

Guaranteed by Good Housekeeping

KEM·GLO® *So Beautiful! So Durable!*

LOOKS and WASHES LIKE BAKED ENAMEL

Here's beauty that makes housekeeping easier! KEM-GLO has a rich subdued lustre. It's so tough even boiling hot water won't harm it. Fruit juices, beverages, cooking spatters, cosmetics, kiddies' crayon drawings . . . wash off as easy as washing your refrigerator. It resists scuffing and chipping, too. That's why KEM-GLO, the miracle lustre enamel, is first choice for kitchen and bathroom walls and ceilings, for all woodwork throughout your home . . . yes, for furniture, too.

It's so easy to apply. Just stir and brush it on. In 3 or 4 hours it's dry. KEM-GLO comes in 16 gorgeously styled colors and a real white white that stays white. Plus hundreds of lovely combinations of intermixed colors.

SUPER KEM-TONE . . . The DeLuxe Easy-to-Use Wall Paint
Repeated Washing Can't Mar Its Matchless Beauty !

America's No. 1 wall paint . . . rich as velvet . . . yet so amazingly durable that repeated washings won't mar its beauty. Ready-to-use, easy-to-apply . . . so quick to dry you can have a "new" room in a day. Lovely colors, matched to KEM-GLO.

$1⁶⁵ QUART $5¹⁹ GALLON
(Deep Colors Slightly Higher)

SUPER KEM-TONE, KEM-GLO AND KEM-TONE ARE SOLD AT LEADING PAINT, HARDWARE, LUMBER AND DEPARTMENT STORES EVERYWHERE

130

NUTRITION?
WHAT NUTRITION?

Sugar Smacks and **Sugar Frosted Flakes** begin to fill our children's cereal bowls.

No-Cal Ginger Ale, the first successful sugar-free soft drink using cyclamates, is launched by Kirsch Beverages.

LESS WORK FOR MOTHER

A new baby formula consisting of evaporated milk, vitamin D and Dextri-Maltose is tested on 57 infants whose weight and general development is normal or in some cases superior.

Pream, a powdered instant cream for coffee, is launched by M & R Dietetic Labs in Ohio.

OY Does This Taste Good Or What

Zion Kosher Meat Products in New York introduces a line of quick-frozen dinners including minute steaks and veal chops.

•

FROZEN PEAS & Q'S

Mr. Birdseye markets the first frozen peas.

•

Chilled To The Crust

Using the same quick-freeze technology developed by Clarence Birdseye, a Chester, New York local baker creates the first frozen bread.

LET-TUS REJOICE IN THIS SNAPPY OCCASION

The U.S. Department of Agriculture wins a gold medal for its development of a new leaf lettuce called **Salad Bowl**, high in vitamin C, and an all-purpose bush snap-bean called **Wade**.

SO SPREADABLE, IT'S INCREDIBLE

Sycova, a new bread spread made from soybeans, is brought to market by Soya Corp. of America.

General Baking Co. has a new type of high-protein, low calorie bread made with celery, pumpkin, carrots and spinach.

GETTING FOODS FAST

Within 15 seconds after dropping coins in the slot, you can have a hamburger, a baked ham sandwich or frank-furter with a new food-vending machine installed at a New York airline terminal.

Molded Fiber Glass Co. manufactures reinforced bread delivery trays for **Wonder Bread**.

1952

As big as a refrigerator and costing over $1,200, *microwave ovens are now available for home use.*

THE BELLS ARE RINGING FOR YOU AND YOUR EGG

You'll now know when your egg is done, thanks to a new sandglass egg timer that rings a bell when it's cooked.

William M. Martin of James Dole Engineering Co. *develops a process for quick, high-temperature steriliza-tion for use in canning fresh milk and other perishables.*

GETTING TO THE CORE OF THE MATTER

Elron Products in Chicago is importing a fruit corer for coring and slicing apples, pears and other fruit.

COOKING IN THE FUTURE WITH NON-STICK KITCHEN UTENSILS

A new greaseless experi-mental muffin tin coated with a plastic called Teflon, which prevents muffins from sticking, is unveiled at the National Plastics Exposition.

Wallpaper can be applied more easily thanks to a new "cut and paste" machine that has recently been patented.

A Buffalo, New York company is offering a low-cost, portable electric room heater with its own thermostatic control.

A LEG UP ON HOUSE WORK
A new slipper-like "foot mop" helps housewives polish or dry mop floors using their gams.

For $1.19, you can now get a quart of floor wax that shines your floor and kills bugs at the same time.

ALL WASHED UP AND DRIED OUT
Bendix introduces a combination clothes washer and built-in hot-air drier in a 3-foot wide unit.

TAKING THE STEAM OUT OF HEAT
Dr. Maria Telkes of Massachusetts Institute of Technology patents a house panel that captures solar heat.

Your thermostat can now be turned on and off automatically by using the new "Morning Comfort," an automatic temperature control device.

Plastron Inc. introduces flower-scented plastic shower and window curtains.

A plastic pool which can hold up to 15 people is the latest in backyard bathing.

A DOLLY OF THEIR OWN
Black children no longer have to play with stereotypical painted dolls for now they have their very own anthropologically correct dolls.

NOT JUST ANOTHER PRETTY COMEDIAN
Comedian Danny Kaye and his manager take out a patent on a new blowup paper toy for children.

IT AIN'T BROKE 'TILL IT'S BROKE
Columbia Records brings out four unbreakable 6" records for children starring among others Yogi Berra and Phil Rizzuto.

Ladies can now have a quick permanent with *BOBBI PIN-CURL* thanks to the GILLETTE CO.

SHIELD, a product that makes fabrics water-repellent, is now available to consumers.

WANT A HOT TIP?
The first filter-tip cigarette to hit the market is brought out by P. LORILLARD CO., makers of *OLD GOLD*.

PROCTER & GAMBLE'S *GLEEM* toothpaste hits the marketplace.

Claiming that its new *ZEST* soap can produce suds even in salt water and leaves no ring around the tub, PROCTER & GAMBLE launches its latest product which sells for $.15 a bar.

THE GREENING OF CONSUMER PRODUCTS
Green chlorophyll is used in almost 100 products including chewing gum, cough drops and toilet paper.

SOME CARS NOW COME EQUIPPED WITH TINTED WINDSHIELDS, AUTOMATIC HEADLAMP DIMMERS AND AUTOMATIC OVERDRIVE.

IMPORTED MOTOR CAR CO. OF HOOPESTON, ILLINOIS HAS A NEW DASHBOARD INDICATOR WHICH ALERTS THE DRIVER TO ELECTRICAL PROBLEMS.

NO MORE GETTING HOT UNDER THE COLLAR

General Motors perfects an air-conditioning unit for cars and says it will be available next year in some of its models at an additional cost of around $500.

AN OIL FOR ALL SEASONS

Standard Oil makes a new year-round motor oil.

THAT'S A LOT OF HORSES

Chrysler unveils the most powerful passenger car engine ever produced in the U.S.— 310 horsepower.

A SCENT OF LEMON, OR VANILLA OR LAVENDER OR CUT GRASS

A chlorophyll kit containing a variety of scents to make your car smell fresh is being sold to garages and commercial car washes.

LET'S HEAR IT FOR THE RED, GREEN & YELLOW

The streets of New York have new three-color traffic lights eliminating the delay between the red and the green.

THE FIRST CAR WITH A PLASTIC BODY rolls out of the Glasspar Co. in Costa Mesa, California.

B.F. GOODRICH CO. develops passenger car tires it says are capable of running safely at sustained speeds of more than 100 mph.

ACCORDING TO "AUTOMOTIVE INDUSTRIES," power-steering will be available in some General Motors cars.

1952

WATERING DOWN THE INK

A fountain pen purported to last up to 18 months by carrying a concentrated ink supply activated by water is put on the market by Elsart Novelties.

Waterman pen *begins marketing "the smoothest writing instrument ever developed"—its $6.00 ballpoint pen with a retractable sapphire tip.*

●

The first video recorder *is demonstrated in Los Angeles.*

Mary Thielen of Scarsdale, N.Y. *invents the teleprompter that displays an actor's lines, stage directions and timing.*

RCA Chairman David Sarnoff *announces the development of the first portable television camera.*

The first 8-mm *sound-on-film projector is introduced by Movie Mite.*

●

ALL ABOARD!

Two new automatic ticket-printing machines go into operation in Manhattan's Grand Central Station.

American Airlines *introduces electronic reservations.*

SHE CAN'T COME TO THE PHONE NOW—HER HAIR ISN'T DONE

A new telephone is unveiled at Britain's National Radio Show which allows you to see the person you are talking to.

BUZZING DR. MALONE BUZZING DR. MALONE

Doctors are now as near as their breast pockets thanks to a new pocket radio pager that sends a vibrating buzz when they are needed.

Bell Telephone demonstrates two new answering machines.

CALLING DICK TRACY CALLING DICK TRACY

A radio, tiny enough to be worn on the wrist, is produced by Western Electric Co. engineers.

The Navy & RCA announce the production of a new radar which can pick up weather and terrain obstacles up to 200 miles in front of an aircraft.

From West Germany comes The Minifon, a small recorder used for dictation by businessmen.

- - - - - - - -

A portable dictating and transcribing machine is developed by Thomas A. Edison Inc.

• For only $2.00 you can now have your very own vial for testing atomic radiation.

• Polaroid Corporation and scientists of the Naval Research Laboratory develop an atomic radiation detector the size of a watch that becomes fluorescent when exposed to radiation.

• **Paint-by-Numbers** appeals to amateur artists.

• Unable to meet the huge demand for *Scrabble*, businessman James Brunot sells out to Selchow & Righter.

COFFEE BREAK AT THE WATER COOLER

A new standard-size water cooler offers coffee or water depending on which button is pressed.

DON'T BLOW THIS ONE OFF

A new inflatable rubber mattress small enough to fit in a soldier's pack is being manufactured by the **B.F. Goodrich Company** for the Armed Forces.

• A non-jamming zipper is manufactured by Manhattan's **Snag-Pruf Zipper Corp.**

REMOVING THE ROAR FROM THE ROLLER RINK

A new plastic wheel designed to remove the noise from roller skating has been developed by **United States Rubber Company and Fo-Matic Enterprises, Inc.**

YES, BUT CAN IT SURVIVE BEING STRAPPED TO THE LEG OF A RUNAWAY ELEPHANT?

The **Elgin National Watch Company** makes a prototype of an electronic wristwatch that carries its own power source and requires no mainspring or winding mechanism, but says it will be years before the watch can be sold at a competitive price.

• **Anchor Manufacturing Company** introduces lightweight four-legged walkers as a walking aid.

• **Sonotone** introduces the first transistor hearing aid in the U.S.

• **Ray-Ban** sunglasses which ban two-way glare are developed by **Bausch & Lomb Optical Co.**

WHAT A YEAR IT WAS!

SCIENCE 1952

THIS ONE DIDN'T GET AWAY

A native fisherman fishing off the coast of the Comoro Islands in the Indian Ocean catches a 5-ft. long coelacanth, a "living fossil" dating back to the Devonian period 300 million years ago.

Jacques Cousteau begins undersea archeology off the coast of Marseille.

An 800-mile canyon is discovered on the floor of the Atlantic Ocean between Bermuda and the Azores.

According to the publisher of Radio-Electronics magazine, electronic testing will be used in the future to determine the compatibility of couples contemplating marriage.

The **MANIAC**, a new calculator which took several years to build, is unveiled at the Los Alamos Scientific Laboratory of the University of California. It is capable of solving a mathematical problem in a half-hour that would take one person with an adding machine two years to solve.

In Chicago, 34 leading scientists attack U.S. anti-Communist visa policy as a danger to science.

AN EXPLOSIVE SUBJECT

April 1st: An atomic device dropped from a plane at Frenchman's Flat testing grounds near Las Vegas, Nevada, producing twin columns of smoke forming a lateral curtain and many tentacles instead of the usual mushroom-shaped cloud, launches a new series of tests and is the 13th explosion at the Nevada proving grounds.

April 15th: The 14th atomic weapon is detonated at the Nevada proving grounds producing a fireball that breaks into two tail-like pieces which join together into a giant ring.

April 22nd: As millions of people across the nation watch the first televised transmission of an atomic test, the most powerful bomb ever exploded within the boundaries of the U.S. and more powerful than those dropped on Hiroshima or Nagasaki is detonated over Yucca Flat.

May 1st: 2,000 marines hunch in foxholes 7,000 yards from "ground zero" when an A-bomb is dropped by a bomber and explodes some 2,000 feet above Yucca Flat.

May 7th: A nuclear device is detonated atop a 300-ft. steel tower at the Nevada proving grounds producing a predawn fireball said to be the brightest of all previous Nevada tests.

May 25th: With 1,000 troops and 600 military observers huddled in foxholes about 7,000 yards away, the 18th and most brilliant nuclear explosion is touched off at Yucca Flat.

June 5th: Using over 700 white mice to test radioactivity, the spring series of atomic tests ends with an atomic weapon detonated atop a 300-ft. steel tower at Yucca Flat.

NOVEMBER: The Atomic Energy Commission announces that the U.S. has exploded the first hydrogen bomb at Eniwetok Atoll, Pacific.

> Details on the 85-ton atomic cannon released by the U.S. Army.

Britain conducts its first atomic test in Monte Bello Islands, 50 miles northwest of Australia, making it the third known nation to possess atomic secrets.

Keel of the U.S.S. "Nautilus," the world's first atomic-powered submarine, is laid by President Truman at Groton, Connecticut.

A radiation laboratory at Livermore, California is approved by the AEC.

The AEC announces it has developed a "scintillating probe" that can detect uranium beneath the earth's surface faster than a Geiger counter.

The world's biggest uranium deposit is discovered in Nigeria.

Uranium is discovered near New York City in Warren County, New Jersey.

In New York, Walter Kidde Nuclear Laboratories is formed to develop commercial uses for atomic energy.

The AEC is going to build a $1.2 billion plant for uranium production on a site 80 miles east of Cincinnati.

The Chalk River research reactor in Ontario is the site of the world's first serious nuclear accident, as almost one million gallons of radioactive water are accidentally released.

Westinghouse Electric is awarded a contract by the AEC for construction of a nuclear power plant suitable for propulsion of large naval vessels such as aircraft carriers.

HONEY, CAN YOU THROW A QUICK STEAK ON THE GRILL?

According to an article published in NATURE, when you hear the warning siren signaling a nuclear attack, quickly drink a cocktail or any alcoholic beverage and eat a steak. This increases your chances of escaping radiation death if the Atomic bomb goes off in your neighborhood.

WHAT A YEAR IT WAS!

ANCIENT DIGS & DISCOVERIES

HIEROGLYPHICS from five Egyptian pyramids dating back 4,000 years indicate that the Egyptians believed the earth was round.

FIT FOR A KING

A French expedition discovers the 3,500-year-old ivory throne of Phoenicia's kings.

Italian archeologists discover a new Venus, sans arms, near Naples in the ruins of Masseria del Gigante.

WELL, NOW, AIN'T THIS THE CAT'S MEOW

192 mummified cats from Egypt dating back to 600-200 B.C. are rediscovered by a zoologist in the vaults of the British Natural History Museum.

A 2,300-year-old pre-Incan city is discovered only ten miles from the center of Lima, Peru.

According to an Oxford University professor, discovery of 25,000,000-year-old fossil bones in Lake Victoria, Africa may show that man is not descended from apelike-animals as reconstruction shows primates who walked on all fours and did not swing from trees like the modern gibbon, supposedly man's ancestor.

Skeletons believed to be the remains of an Indian culture more than 8,000 years old are discovered on Santa Rosa Island, California.

USING CHARCOAL ANALYSIS, PROFESSOR W.F. LIBBY OF THE UNIVERSITY OF CHICAGO DATES **STONEHENGE**, THE FINEST MEGALITHIC MONUMENT IN BRITAIN, TO APPROXIMATELY 1848 B.C.

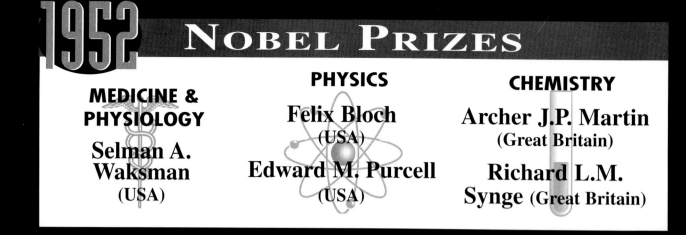

1952 NOBEL PRIZES

MEDICINE & PHYSIOLOGY
Selman A. Waksman
(USA)

PHYSICS
Felix Bloch
(USA)

Edward M. Purcell
(USA)

CHEMISTRY
Archer J.P. Martin
(Great Britain)

Richard L.M. Synge (Great Britain)

German rocket scientist WERNHER VON BRAUN suggests that the time has come to begin space exploration and suggests the construction of a space vehicle with Mars as its destination.

Hydrogen, lightest of all elements and one of the atomic fuels that keep stars burning, is discovered in the atmospheres of planets Uranus and Neptune.

Following new series of sightings of "flying saucers," the U.S. Air Force announces that the objects are not a menace to the U.S. and that they have been unable to establish the existence of these objects.

L 886-6 MAKES ITS DEBUT
Located in the winter-evening Milky Way, 25 light years away from earth, the smallest known star is discovered by DR. WILLIAM J. LUYTEN, professor of astronomy at the University of Minneosta, and DR. E.F. CARPENTER, director of the Steward observatory at the University of Arizona.

Hoping to test Einstein's theory of relativity, a total eclipse of the sun lasting 3 minutes, 9 1/2 seconds is viewed and photographed by 70 scientists from ten nations near Khartoum, Anglo-Egyptian Sudan.

Northwestern University's Dearborn Observatory lecturer JOHN STERNIG believes that space travel will become a reality before the end of the 20th Century.

Using its new cosmotron, the Brookhaven National Laboratory produces a beam of protons with energies of 2,300,000,000-ev, the first time an atom-smasher exceeds the 1,000,000,000-ev mark.

Joshua Lederberg learns that viruses can transmit genetic material from one cell to another which represents an important step toward genetic engineering.

Dr. Andrew M. Gleason, 31-year-old assistant professor of math at Harvard, receives the $1,000 Newcomb Cleveland Prize for coming up with a solution to a problem in abstract geometry that stumped mathematicians for over 50 years.

The first general assembly of the International Mathematical Union is held in Rome, Italy.

WHAT A YEAR IT WAS!

Medicine

IT'S NOT MY DOGGIE

Dog bites should receive the same treatment as other flesh wounds which includes washing with soap and water, removal of dead tissue and stitching up the wound.

WATCH OUT FOR THOSE COW PADDIES

Texas authorizes loans to medical students who agree to practice in rural areas for five years.

The nation is experiencing a critical shortage of nurses.

SUCH A PAIN YOU SHOULDN'T KNOW FROM

- Jewish doctors from all over the world convene in Jerusalem to discuss medical problems arising out of the mass immigration to Israel.

- Dr. Charles E. Dutchess, medical director of Schenley Laboratories, predicts that within the lifetime of many Americans alive today, a tenth of the population will live to be 100 or older with active people of 85+ comprising a substantial number in every community.

- Approximately one million people in the U.S. have diabetes and are unaware of their medical problem.

- Chronic alcoholism is the fourth highest cause of death in the U.S. with only heart disease, cancer and tuberculosis ahead.

- Psychiatry, not prostitution, appears to be the oldest profession in the world according to anthropologist George Peter Murdock of Yale University.

- According to two doctors at Montreal's McGill University, the most effective treatment for frostbite is immersion in a warm bath.

THE NATION GETS BUGGED

The U.S. experiences its first widespread epidemic of influenza B infection since 1945-46.

The Euthanasia Society of America petitions the U.N. to establish the right of incurably ill people to a merciful death.

The *Journal of the American Medical Association* reports a cancer patient hit a fever of 114 degrees— one of the highest temperatures recorded in a human who survived.

To sustain good mental and physical prowess, a good breakfast is absolutely essential.

"I treat 'em rough but Atlas Tires can take it!"

says William D. Decker of Pine Bush, N. Y.

"I drive a '37 sedan in the Catskill Mountains on construction jobs and general repair work. Usually the car is 'way overloaded with heavy tools, lumber and bags of cement. Believe me, it's tough going. That's why I use Atlas Tires—they last and last and last!

"What's more, that wide, flat tread grips tight—takes me safely over those steep, winding mountain roads."

Your neighborhood Atlas dealer has Atlas Grip-Safe* and low-pressure Cushionaire* Tires. See him today!

ATLAS*
TIRES · BATTERIES
ACCESSORIES

38,000 ATLAS DEALERS SERVING MOTORISTS EVERYWHERE

*REG. U. S. PAT. OFF. COPYRIGHT 1952, ATLAS SUPPLY COMPANY, NEWARK 2, N. J.

State Of SURGERY 1952

SEPARATED BUT EQUAL

Siamese twins are separated in an unprecedented operation lasting 12 hours and 20 minutes performed by a team of a dozen surgeons at the University of Illinois Research and Educational Hospital in Chicago.

BUT DOCTOR, WHY DO I MOO EVERY TIME I BLOW MY NOSE?

Cartilage from the breastbones of young cattle is being used by plastic surgeons to make new noses, chins, foreheads and other damaged parts of the face.

IN THE FIRST HUMAN TRANSPLANT OF AN ORGAN from a living donor, a French mother gives one of her kidneys to her son but his body rejects the kidney and he dies of uremia a little over a month later.

A NEW OPERATION IS BEING PERFORMED wherein a metal or plastic device is attached to a hip that will not heal.

LET THE DROOLING BEGIN

In the first large-scale test of mass surgery designed to help the insane, 228 patients receive transorbital lobotomies performed in West Virginia by Dr. Walter Freeman of Washington.

THE OPERATION WAS A SUCCESS

A team of nine doctors, five nurses and two technicians participate in an operation at Pennsylvania Hospital in Philadelphia using the first mechanical heart which keeps the patient alive for 80 minutes.

- A 30-year-old woman is the recipient of the first plastic heart valve in an operation performed by Dr. Charles Hufnagel at Georgetown University Hospital.

- Lowering five-year-old Jackie Johnson's body temperature to 79 degrees, the first successful open-heart surgery is carried out by a medical team at the University of Minnesota.

- As a result of massaging the heart, injecting stimulants and applying artificial respiration, a man undergoing chest surgery at Boston City Hospital recovers after his heart stops beating for 25 minutes

TAKING THIS STATISTIC TO HEART

Four times as many people die of heart disease or other diseases of the circulatory system than die of cancer.

The electric pacemaker, designed to regulate an irregular heart rhythm, is introduced into the medical community.

In monitoring 70 heart disease patients, the mortality rate is higher for those who are restricted to bed than those patients who sit in a comfortable chair with their feet in a down position.

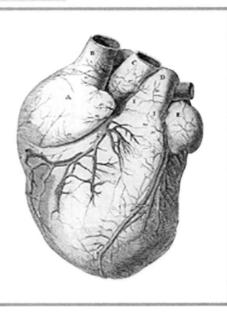

In an article published in *Modern Medicine*, Dr. Walter Alvarez states that the female sex hormone estrogen has been successful in reducing hardening of the arteries in male chicks on high cholesterol diets and that the hormone has been wrongly blamed for breast and uterine cancer in women.

The Journal of the American Medical Association publishes an article indicating that male heart attack victims have a 95% chance of surviving for more than five years and a very good chance of living more than ten years.

Harvard's Paul Zoll is the first to use electric shock to treat cardiac arrest.

WHAT A YEAR IT WAS!

1952

POLIO • POLIO • POLIO • POLIO

The U.S. suffers its worst polio epidemic since 1949 with about 50,000 new cases reported, the largest number hitting Texas. ● The prevention of polio may some day be possible as a major breakthrough in laboratory experiments shows promise. The University of Pennsylvania publishes research showing that human milk has a nitrogen-containing sugar not present in all cow's milk and it appears to increase resistance to some viral diseases including poliomyelitis. ● The National Foundation of Infantile Paralysis announces that after a three-year study it has concluded that there are only three viruses that cause polio. ● The first experimental inoculation on humans with live poliomyelitis virus is reported.

CANCER

• An estimated 220,000 people die this year from cancer.

• The number of deaths from cancer has increased all over the world.

• Cancer is being treated more effectively by beaming powerful 2-million-volt X-rays at the tumor while the patient is slowly turned in a rotating chair.

• Removal of both adrenal glands in patients with advanced breast or prostrate cancer has shown dramatic results in about 50% of patients at the University of Chicago.

• Drs. T.C. Davison and A.H. Letton of Atlanta tell the International College of Surgeons that if women could be trained to examine their own breasts for lumps once a month, there would be a major reduction in the death rate from this type of cancer.

• The Children's Cancer Research Foundation opens the "Jimmy Fund" clinic in Boston dedicated to the research and treatment of cancer in children.

THE SMOKING LUNG

In a recently released study on the correlation between smoking and cancer of the bronchus, statistics show that 87% of men with this disease are very heavy smokers and only 2% are nonsmokers with smokers having a 50 times greater chance of developing lung cancer than their nonsmoking counterparts.

DRUGS

• Critically ill tuberculosis patients get new hope with the introduction of three new drugs—Rimifon, Nydrazid and Marsilid.

• A new time-release capsule called a "Spansule" containing 100 tiny pellets which releases medication periodically is developed by Smith, Kline & French Laboratories.

• Vitamin B6 is found to be an effective treatment for sciatica, facial neuralgia and other diseases of the peripheral nervous system.

• Severe allergy reactions are being successfully treated with a combination of procaine and vitamin C.

• Spanish doctors report remarkable results in treating rheumatoid arthritis through injections of nitrogen mustard.

• Compound F, a cortisone derivative, has been found to relieve joint pain associated with arthritis, bursitis and osteoarthritis.

• 30 out of 33 people who receive weekly injections of vitamin B12 for up to three weeks feel relief from symptoms of osteoarthritis for as long as five months after treatment stops.

• Conclusive evidence indicates that continued use of barbiturates results in addiction, contrary to former beliefs that these drugs just act as non-habit-forming sedatives.

• Seeds from an Egyptian plant called "Ammi maius Linn" are being used to treat patients with vitiligo, a condition in which the skin loses pigment.

• Radioactive iodine is being used successfully in the treatment of thyroid conditions.

142

HEADACHES

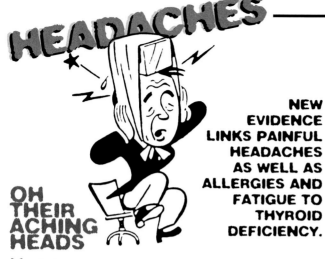

OH THEIR ACHING HEADS

NEW EVIDENCE LINKS PAINFUL HEADACHES AS WELL AS ALLERGIES AND FATIGUE TO THYROID DEFICIENCY.

Headaches generally are more common among women, young adults, single people, executives and professional groups.

85% of medical students suffer from headaches with executives following at 77.3% and clerical workers logging in at 68.2%.

There is no scientific evidence that wearing tight hats or living under great tension causes baldness according to Dr. Herbert Rattner of Northwestern University.

Doctors at New York's Montefiore Hospital report that emotional stimulation, not eyestrain, is the cause of the increasing number of tension headaches among children who watch television.

THE PRICE OF EXCELLENCE

Migraine headaches, dubbed *"the disease of the alert mind"* seem to afflict people with high I.Q.'s and mostly women who share the following general profile:

Well-educated

Alert

Sharp, eager personality

Short

Trim figure

Attractive

Bright, intelligent face

Moves and acts quickly

Perfectionistic

Leader

Plans work far in advance and makes sure it is done quickly and perfectly

DENTISTRY

GET OUT THOSE CHOCOLATES AND CELEBRATE

Experiments conducted at the University of Wisconsin indicate that cereals made of processed oat, wheat and corn foods are harder on teeth than diets high in sugar.

- The A.M.A. deems fluoridation of water safe and directly related to the reduction of tooth decay in children.

- Approximately 22,000,000 people in the U.S. wear some form of removable dentures.

- As a result of diseases of the gum and bone structure, one out of every two men will either lose all his teeth or will show signs of disease by age 45.

- A Northwestern University pediatrician recommends that "baby teeth" be brushed after every meal beginning at 18 months and visits to the dentist begin by age two.

- An article published in the "Journal of the American Dental Association" indicates that children who breathe through their mouths run the risk of developing chronic inflammation of the gums which could lead to loss of teeth in young adults.

1952

Women in early stages of pregnancy should avoid X-rays as they cause birth defects.

CHILDBIRTH

STALKING THE STORK

"California Medicine" reports that a comparison of actual birth dates with dates predicted by doctors in Palo Alto shows only one forecast in 40 to be accurate and that the baby's arrival date will probably be later than earlier.

THE HIGHER THE SCORE THE BETTER

The "Apgar Score" that will often reveal prenatal problems and birthing injuries is developed by Virginia Apgar and includes checking the infant's pulse, reflexes, respiration, color and muscle tone.

ACCURACY WITHIN SPITTING DISTANCE

Dr. Gustav William Rapp of Loyola University School of Dentistry and Dr. Garwood C. Richardson of Northwestern University Medical School develop a technique for determining the sex of an unborn child by testing the saliva of the expectant mother.

IS SHE OR ISN'T SHE—ONLY HER DOCTOR KNOWS FOR SURE

Using a sample of mucus from the patient's cervix, a new pregnancy test with a 99% accuracy rate has been developed by Dr. Maxwell Roland of New York University-Bellevue Medical Center.

GIVING THE BABY A BREATHING ROOM

Doctors Hospital in Seattle, Washington introduce a lifesaving device for premature babies known as an air lock resuscitator.

According to the Metropolitan Life Insurance Company, the first day of life is the most dangerous within the first year as one-third of all deaths occur on the day of birth with three-fifths taking placing during the first week of life.

With 150,000 babies a year dying at childbirth or shortly after, most of whom are premature, doctors recommend that the gestation period be the full nine months if possible.

A study of Hiroshima victims by Japanese doctors reveals that atomic radiation does not render women permanently sterile.

Professional and managerial parents appear to give birth to boys who average one inch taller in height and three pounds heavier than those born of unskilled or semi-skilled parents.

Accidents rank first as cause of death among children and young people between the ages of 1 to 24.

In a $500,000 research project of the National Foundation for Infantile Paralysis, 35,000 children are inoculated in Houston, Texas, half of whom receive gamma globulin and the other half receive gelatin.

Healthier babies are born to mothers who eat more meat during their pregnancy according to the University of Chicago Lying-in Hospital.

First contraceptive pill is developed.

THERE'S NO PLACE LIKE HOME

About 28,000 people die each year in accidents in the home centering around the bedroom, kitchen and stairs.

Evidence indicates that the average height of Americans is increasing.

Bonn University medical officials announce the successful treatment of rheumatism, sciatica, lumbago and mild arthritis with ultrasound waves directed to the affected parts of the body.

An article appearing in *The New York Times* reveals that progesterone and estrogen hormones given to virgin heifers resulted in them producing milk without having had calves.

A report by Alfred Hershey and Martha Chase confirming that DNA holds hereditary data is released.

Birth and brain injuries are being recognized as a major cause of epilepsy.

Persistent coughing could be the result of a hair pressing against the eardrum.

The definition of a "normal" person is an adult who focuses their energy on main problems.

GETTING THE FAT IN

Researchers at the Highland Alameda County Hospital in Oakland, California report that arthritis patients on a high-fat diet showed significant improvement in their symptoms but the pain returned when they put starch and sugar back into their diet.

Statistics based on the deaths of 50,000 people released by the Metropolitan Life Insurance Company show that the death rate is 50% higher for overweight people than persons with normal weight in the same age group.

YOU BETTER LAY OFF THOSE FRENCH FRIES

An estimated 25% to 30% of the adult population of the U.S. is overweight with overweight women in the 50-70 age group expected to reach as high as 60%.

Research at University of California reveals that little girls learn to lie earlier than little boys.

Surveys conducted at DePaul University indicate that men are bigger liars than women.

FLATTERY WILL GET YOU EVERYWHERE

Girls are charmed by flattery even at a very young age.

According to studies at the University of Minnesota, women who diet excessively risk losing their sex appeal.

Girls who wear sunglasses during the day appear to have improved vision at night.

Scientists believe that women are less inclined to insomnia because their nightly cosmetic routine helps them put the day's fast pace behind them.

A U.S. Public Health survey reveals that although women live longer than men, they experience more bad health.

Got the hiccups?

Two Boston doctors suggest you try the kitchen treatment. Blow into a paper bag, hold your breath and the excessive amount of carbon dioxide accumulated in the body could very well do the trick.

Life and Health has an article on how to live with an ulcer:

1. Eat your meals the same time every day.

2. Prepare foods simply. Easy on the condiments.

3. Avoid hot foods, alcoholic beverages and tobacco.

4. Sleep at least 8 to 10 hours.

5. Leave your work at the office and avoid overtime.

6. Enjoy your home life.

7. Avoid games or sports that create tension.

PASSINGS

Australian **Sister Elizabeth Kenny**, who went against the standard polio treatment of her day and cured until-then incurable patients, dies at age 66 after a long bout with Parkinson's. Sister Kenny fought against doctors on several continents, and eventually her heat therapy method was used in Australia, America and other countries.

Leading German-born psychoanalyst **Dr. Karen Horney**, a founder of the American Institute for Psychoanalysis, dies at age 67.

Business 1952

The New York Stock Exchange

The New York Stock Exchange closes at 281.08—the highest number since 1930.

The Exchange ceases Saturday trading.

America has approximately 16 million stockholders. Almost 8 1/2 million women own stock, while only 7 1/2 million men own stock. 52% of stockholders of approximately 1,000 large companies are women.

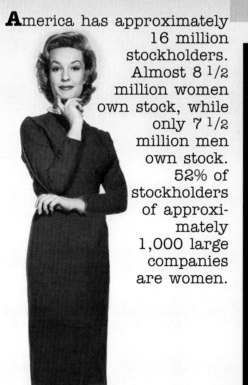

National Gross Product
$344 billion, $500 million

The Consumer's Price Index
reaches a new all-time high of 190.8.

The new Series H Savings Bond is issued, offering 3% interest if held to maturity.

Approximately $30 billion in U.S. currency is in circulation.

One-sixth of all companies in the United States are somehow related to automobiles.

Roughly three million women work part-time. Some professions that work well with a woman's flexible schedule include tutor, typist, copywriter, saleswoman, therapist, waitress, secretary, cashier, riveter, switchboard operator, dental hygienist, bookkeeper, nurse and stenographer.

WHAT A YEAR IT WAS!

147

Old soldier **Douglas MacArthur** becomes chairman of the board of **Remington Rand, Inc.** with a $100,000 yearly salary.

Coca-Cola opens a plant in Cork, Irish Republic.

The first **Holiday Inn** hotel opens in Memphis, Tennessee.

Shopping without going into stores becomes a reality as *"The Family Shopper"* magazine allows consumers to send money to a local store, which then forwards the order to the manufacturer, eliminating the need for salespeople and inventory.

Cadillac celebrates its golden anniversary.

E.I. du Pont de Nemours & Co. celebrates its 150th anniversary.

For the first time in over 50 years, the boss of **Macy's New York** is not a member of the founding Straus family.

Italian **Vespa** scooters invade the American marketplace, and thousands are sold by **Sears, Roebuck & Co.**

An eight-month-old baby, perhaps the youngest defendant in the country, plus 185 other members of the du Pont family are defendants in a federal antitrust case.

Antitrust suits are filed by the Justice Department against IBM, Procter & Gamble and Colgate-Palmolive-Peet.

Inventor Harry Ferguson wins over $9 million from Ford Motor Company for a patent violation suit.

famous birth
Christie Hefner

PASSINGS

His name synonymous with healthy baby food **Frank Gerber**, co-founder of Gerber Products Co., dies at age 79.

•

The presidents of the two most powerful unions in the U.S. die within twelve days of each other. President of the CIO since 1940, Scottish-born **Phillip Murray** dies of a heart attack at age 66. Earlier in the year Murray oversaw the steelworkers' strike, effecting 650,000 union members. President of the AFL for nearly three decades, **William Green** dies at age 79. Green was against the Taft-Hartley Act, Communists in his union and was a staunch supporter of President Harry S. Truman.

1952 ADVERTISEMENT

Solving BIG, BIG, BIG *problems*
(and small ones, too)

The Burroughs Sensimatic "300" with 11 totals is the newest of the new Sensimatic accounting machines . . . with versatility enough to handle all of the most complicated accounting jobs . . . and with a pleasantly uncomplicated price!

Series 300

Solving BIG, BIG *problems*
(requiring 5 totals or less)

The Burroughs Sensimatic "200" is the best answer for businesses that need a five-total accounting machine for figure-facts and records. It's got big-machine versatility . . . small-machine simplicity . . . and a medium-machine price!

Series 200

Solving BIG *problems*
(60% of all accounting jobs)

First of the Sensimatic accounting machines, the Burroughs Sensimatic "100" covers most of the accounting work of most business. It's just as fast, flexible, easy to use as the other Sensimatics—and it costs so little!

Series 100

Now there are THREE !

Burroughs Sensimatic
Accounting machines

With the introduction of the new Burroughs Sensimatic "300", there's the right Sensimatic for every size business . . . for every size problem. Each of these modern accounting tools is the fastest and simplest in its field. Each has a sensing unit to direct it through every accounting job automatically . . . to give it almost unlimited versatility. And each costs far less than you'd expect to pay for such a machine. See the Sensimatic that's right for your business . . . call your Burroughs man today. Burroughs Adding Machine Company, Detroit 32, Michigan.

B Burroughs

149

1952
UNION NEWS

475 strikes are started in April alone. 475 are also started in October.

The nation is crippled by a 53-day steel strike by the CIO United Steelworkers, which effects over 600,000 workers, costs approximately $4 billion and drastically reduces steel production. Trying to avoid a strike, **President Truman** seizes the steel industry, but the Supreme Court rules his action unconstitutional. President Truman refuses to invoke the Taft-Hartley Act, and blames the greed of the major steel companies as the cause of the strike. During the strike, which costs $40 million a day, **John L. Lewis** offers workers a $10 million loan. The strikers win a $.16 hour raise plus additional benefits.

Due to President Truman overruling the Wage Stabilization Board, 270,000 members of the United Mine Workers are granted a $1.90 raise instead of the suggested $1.50.

The advice AFL American Federation of Musicians President **James C. Petrillo** offers to delegates at a convention in Santa Barbara, California is "Think more, strike less."

The AFL Sailors Union of the Pacific strike for 62 days, eventually receiving a 5% pay raise.

90,000 CIO Oil Workers strike for a $.25 an hour raise.

60,000 Italian miners strike.

Guatemala legalizes 335 unions.

The longest strike of 1952 is for 17 weeks by AFL Pressmen and CIO Guildmen against the *Tacoma News Tribune*.

Railroad companies and unions finally settle a three-year dispute, and 150,000 workers are given raises. President Truman commands the Army, which had been operating the railroads for 21 months, to return them to their rightful owners.

AFL Insurance Agents International members working at Prudential Insurance Co. strike for 81 days in 32 states.

CIO United Auto Workers strike for ten weeks against International Harvester Company in Melrose Park, Illinois. Non-striking worker **William Foster** is beaten to death at another International Harvester plant after crossing a picket line.

WHAT A YEAR IT WAS!

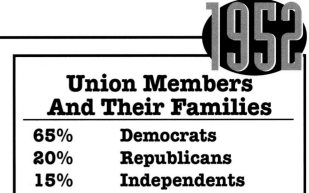

STRIKE. STOP. GET BACK TO WORK. STOP. OR ELSE. STOP.

30,000 AFL Commercial Telegraphers Union workers across the country employed by Western Union strike for 52 days and get a reduced work week of forty hours.

Union Members And Their Families

65%	Democrats
20%	Republicans
15%	Independents

George Meany is elected president of the AFL following the death of president **William Green**. **Walter Reuther** is elected president of the CIO after the death of longtime president **Philip Murray**.

AFL President **George Meany** urges repeal of the Taft-Hartley Act.

In a novel way to lure workers from a rival, the AFL electrical workers send striptease artists to members of the CIO Communications Union.

The Supreme Court rules against the St. Louis-San Francisco Railway and the Brotherhood of Railroad Trainmen for ignoring the Railway Labor Act and hiring whites to replace already-employed black train porters.

The National Negro Labor Committee is formed to protect black workers' rights.

Workers For Stevenson Unite!

Adlai Stevenson is endorsed by the AFL and the CIO.

New Yorkers will not be danish-less, since 6,000 bakery truck drivers win a weekly pay raise of $6.

AFL Screen Extras Guild wins new salaries—$25 for swimmers and dancers.

60 countries attend the 35th meeting of the International Labor Conference in Geneva, Switzerland.

53 million workers in 70 countries are members of the International Confederation of Free Trade Unions.

WHAT A YEAR IT WAS!

151

DELECTABLES

	$ .04
Apples (lb.)	.10
Avocados (each)	.10
Bananas (lb.)	.15
Bell Peppers (lb.)	.27
Bosco	.23
Boysenberries (lb.)	.20
Bread (loaf)	

Peanut Butter	$ .35
Rhubarb (lb.)	.19
Rutabagas (lb.)	.07
Sugar (lb.)	.10
Swiss Cheese (lb.)	.55
Syrup	.27
Tomatoes (lb.)	.08
Wheatena	.19

Broccoli (lb.)	
Butter (lb.)	$ .10
Candy Bar	.85
Carrots (bunch)	.10
Cheddar Cheese (lb.)	.05
Coffee (lb.)	.59
Corn (ear)	.77
Cottage Cheese	.03
Cranberry Sauce	.23
Eggs (dozen)	.23
Fig Newtons	.47
Grapefruit (lb.)	.43
Grapes (lb.)	.05
Lettuce (head)	.07
Mayonnaise	.06
Oranges (lb.)	.52
Pancake Mix	.03
	.19

FOR THE YOUNG'UNS

Baby Bottle	$ .25
Baby Food (14 jars)	1.00
Baseball Glove	8.75
Bubble Bath	.07
Diapers (pack of six)	.98
Electric Train Set	12.95
Private College (yearly)	900.00
Red Wagon	9.95
Similac Baby Formula	.99
Teddy Bear	2.95

FOR HIM

Briefcase	$ 22.95
Comb	.05
Haircut	1.00
Necktie	2.00
Shoes	17.94
Socks	.85
Stetson Hat	10.00
Suit	98.00
Underwear	.19

FOR HER

Blouse	$ 5.95
Cashmere Sweater	21.95
Eisenhower Jacket	12.95
Gloves	2.98
Hand Cream	.98
Lipstick	1.00
Movado Bracelet Watch	270.00
Petticoat	3.98
Shoes	8.95-14.95
Slacks	17.98
Stockings	1.65
Taffeta Skirt	14.95
Wool Suit	65.00

HOME & HEARTH

Broom	$ .98
Can Opener	.19
Detergent	.27
Dining Rm. Table & 4 Chairs	179.50
Dishwasher	219.95
Dresser	81.95
Dryer	299.95
File Cabinet	37.50
Hair Dryer	7.95
Heating Blanket	36.50
Hot Water Bottle	.79
Ivory Soap	.05
Lamp	25.75
Ottoman	39.50
Pillowcase	.84

HOME & HEARTH

Record Player	$ 12.95
Refrigerator	279.95
Rocking Chair	39.75
Scale	7.95
Shag Carpet (sq. yard)	5.95
Teakettle	22.95
Tissues	.23
Trivet	.99
TV (20")	269.95
Wallpaper (roll)	.99
Wastebasket	3.95
Water Heater	76.95

ENTERTAINMENT

45 rpm Record	$ .89
Hockey Game	.70
Hotel, Miami Beach	14.00
Movie Admission	.50 adults; .20 kids
New York City Opera	1.50 - 3.60

WHAT A YEAR IT WAS!

Now...November Values at REXALL
Drug Stores Everywhere

DON'T MISS AMOS 'N' ANDY'S 10,000th BROADCAST...an event unprecedented in radio history...a milestone in radio enjoyment...Sunday, November 16, 7:30 PM, EST, on CBS RADIO NETWORK for REXALL.

DEEP-CUT BARGAINS
November 5 through 22 only

SPECIAL OFFER!

BISMA-REX POWDER and **BISMA-REX MINT-FLAVORED TABLETS**
Reg. 94¢ VALUE   NOW ONLY **69¢**

Here's a real bargain buy for prompt, prolonged relief from acid-indigestion. For the price of the Powder alone, you get both forms of Rexall's famous Bisma-Rex antacid formula: the Powder, for home use, plus 36 tasty easy-to-take Tablets, for purse or pocket. It's the Value of the Month!

½ POUND MILK CHOCOLATE CHIPS
Special **39¢**
Delicious honeycomb chips coated with smooth, rich milk chocolate. In flavor-sealed package.

Roxbury HOT WATER BOTTLE
ONLY **88¢**
You'd expect to pay up to $1.29! Made of fine quality rubber for years of dependable service.

STAG PARLAY COMBINATION $2.00 Value NOW **$1.19**
"Mint Freeze" After-Shave Stick
"Mint Freeze" Deodorant Stick
Refreshing, frosty-fresh, icy cool! Gets you off to a winning start.

Over ⅓ Off REX-RAY INFRA-RED LAMP Reg. $1.69 Now **$1.09**
Low glare. Soothing heat helps relieve winter's aches and pains.

ELKAY'S AEROSOL AIR REFRESHER
Push-button spray kills cooking, bathroom, garbage and pet odors; clears smoke in seconds.
5 Oz. Reg. 98¢   ONLY **69¢**

REXALL DRUG PRODUCTS ARE GUARANTEED TO GIVE SATISFACTION OR YOUR MONEY BACK

Taking Vitamins? Take the Kind That Give You 3 Big Extras...Plus Red Vitamin B₁₂

REXALL PLENAMINS
Give yourself the plus-protection of REXALL PLENAMINS, the multi-vitamin capsules that give you MORE than the minimum daily requirements of every vitamin with known minimums ...PLUS Liver Concentrate, Iron, and Folic Acid ...PLUS red Vitamin B₁₂. Plenamins are potency-protected by an airtight foilwrap. Simply tear off the daily dose and all the rest remain sanitarily sealed against light, air and moisture.
72's 36-Day Supply **$2.59**

Rexall Mi-31,	tangy, amber-color mouthwash, gargle, all-purpose antiseptic, pint	**79¢**
Rexall Hydrogen Peroxide,	cleans cuts, abrasions, USP 3%, 10 vol., 4 oz.	**18¢**
Cottage Chocolates,	rich, tasty creams, chewies, chips, 1 pound	**$1.10**
Rexall Aspirin,	no faster-acting aspirin made. Bottle of 100 5-grain tablets	**54¢**
Stag Shave Cream,	Coolated or Bay Rum, for "no-scrape" shaving, jumbo tube	**40¢**
Ronson Lighters,	handsome and durable, assorted styles, from	**$6.95**

Christmas Cards

America's Biggest Value | Worth $2.50 | BOX **98¢**
50 handsome cards with glittery snow, colorful trim. Less than 2¢ each.

Imperial Box | Worth $2.30 | BOX **79¢**
18 extra-large cards. All different. Many with gold leaf or metallic foil.

25 Special Christmas Cards, each different and beautifully styled, complete with envelopes. $1.25 value.........49¢
Symphony De Luxe Christmas Cards, 14 different cards printed on smart pebble-grain paper. Gold or silver designs......98¢

You'll Like These New Rexall Products

Rexall PLASTIC QUIK-BANDS 27's **39¢**
These flexible, elastic bandages cling easily and comfortably...even on knuckles! Flesh color, waterproof, oil-and-grease-resistant.

Rexall LOZOTHRICIN Throat Lozenges **69¢**
Now...fast, effective relief from irritated throat. Combines pain-relief of Aspirin and the antibiotic action of Tyrothricin. Cherry-menthol-flavored.

Better, More Complete Relief from Colds Rexall ANAPAC 15's **49¢**
Combines antihistamine with time-tested APC Compound...quickly relieves cold symptoms, plus headache, muscular soreness and fever.

American Custom CHOCOLATES 1 lb. **$2.00**
Our finest! Deluxe assortment of milk and dark chocolates, distinctively boxed.

CARA NOME HAND CREAM 4 oz. **$1.10**
Pure, mild, safe for most sensitive skins, it's hypo-allergenic. Economy 10-oz. size, $2.20.

EVERYDAY NEEDS
Cascade Ink Tablets or Envelopes ....10¢
Adrienne Professional Style Hair Brush......98¢
Stag Lather Brush, natural or nylon bristles, 98¢
Antique Crush Writing Paper, 40 white sheets, 24 envelopes, embossed finish ....98¢
Filler Paper, 2 or 3 punch, generous count, 25¢
Rexall Deluxe Tooth Brush, 6 approved styles, including popular fine-texture nylon ...59¢
Maximum Hard Rubber Pocket Comb, 5-inch..19¢
Electrex Wet-Proof Heating Pad, 3-speed switch, flannel cover, UL approved...$4.98

REXALL REMEDIES
Rexall Milk of Magnesia, pure, mild, creamy-smooth; less "earthy" taste, full pint...39¢
Rexall Nasal-Ator, inhaler for nasal congestion; easy to use, handy to carry ......47¢
Rexall Antihistamine, prompt relief from cold symptoms, 25 mg. tablets, bottle of 15, 39¢
Monacet APC Tablets, for pain relief, 25's ..29¢
Rexall Analgesic Balm, quick, soothing relief from pain or soreness, 1-oz. tube ......49¢

VITAMIN VALUES
Brewer's Yeast Tablets, Vitamin B₁, B₂,100's..39¢
Rexall Cod Liver Oil, high potency, pint...$1.39
Rexall Polydrops, liquid concentrate for babies; mix with formula, milk, juices, 10cc. ..81¢
Rexall Yeast & Iron Tablets, 100's ......59¢
Rexall Polymulsion, child's liquid vitamins, $1.15

MEDICINE CHEST NEEDS
Alco-Rex, cooling alcohol body-rub, pint ..49¢
Rexall Boric Acid, powder or crystals, 4 oz..33¢
Rexall Aspirin for Children, fast-acting, orange-flavored; 50 one-grain tablets, 35¢
Glycerin Suppositories, adult or infant, 12's, 43¢
Rexall Eyelo, soothing, cleansing lotion for irritated eyes; half-pint with eye-cup ..59¢
Rexall Mineral Oil, heavy body, non-fattening, non-habit-forming, full pint ....69¢
Defender Nose and Throat Atomizer ....89¢
Quik-Tel Fever Thermometer, oral or rectal, easy-to-read, accurate $1.55
Stag Lip Aid, for sore, chapped lips........39¢

TOILETRIES
Cara Nome Indelible Lipsticks, 10 shades ..$1.10
Cara Nome Compressed Face Powder, smooths on evenly—without water, clings for hours, in 4 glamorous shades....... $1.10
Cara Nome Cold or Cleansing Cream, 3 oz., $1.10
"84-80" Nail Polish Remover, 3 oz.....29¢
Stag Hair Oil, pleasantly scented, 3 oz. ....40¢

FIRST AID HELPS
Rexall Pro-Cap Adhesive Tape, sticks better, is less irritating; waterproof, ½" x 5 yds., 20¢
Rexall Quik-Pads, ready to use bandages ..33¢
Rexall Mercurochrome, with applicator, ½ oz.,25¢
Rexall Tincture Iodine, with applicator, 1 oz., 17¢
Rexall First Aid Kit, 7 basic needs and First Aid Manual in handy metal kit.......$1.25

YOU CAN DEPEND ON ANY DRUG PRODUCT THAT BEARS THE NAME REXALL

Right reserved to limit quantities. Prices subject to Federal Excise Tax where applicable. Items, prices and dates may vary slightly in Canada. Rexall Drug Company, Los Angeles 48, California.

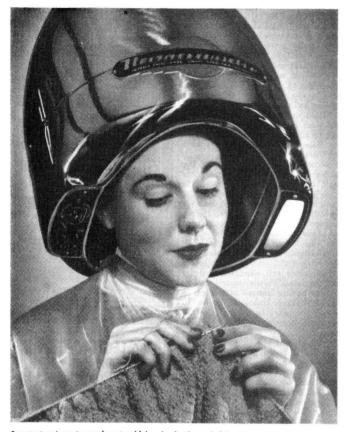

Beauty treatments are less torrid in air that's cooled by TRANE equipment.

Hot blasts and cold drafts are equalized for comfort by TRANE installations.

FROM BEAUTY SHOP TO WELDING SHOP

TRANE air conditioning serves everywhere

Built-to-prescription temperatures for every business in the directory pose no problem for TRANE heating, ventilating, air conditioning and heat transfer equipment.

Some want it cool, others want it warm; still others require indoor climates which run up *and* down the temperature scale.

In their homes, people with every manner of temperature preference, turn to TRANE for

heating equipment which will keep them supremely comfortable in even the most outrageous winter weather.

In service shops, novelty stores and trade schools . . . in manufacturing plants and large commercial buildings all over the country . . . TRANE air conditioning, heating and ventilating equipment reduces worker fatigue and makes for greater alertness and efficiency.

In a word, the proper heating and conditioning of air is TRANE's business. And in the course of minding its business, TRANE serves everywhere.

With the extensive TRANE line from which to choose, complete systems can be developed to fit every heating, ventilating and air conditioning need. There are more than 80 TRANE sales offices in the U.S. They will gladly work with your architect, consulting engineer and contractor.

A free copy of "Choose Your Own Weather" can help you with worthwhile suggestions. Please write for it.

Novelty Stores build more traffic when properly air conditioned. Correct combinations of the many TRANE heating and air conditioning products are available for every type of building.

Training Schools, whether military or civilian, need properly tempered atmosphere if students are to make the right kind of progress. TRANE Unit Ventilators serve schools everywhere.

Modern Buildings afford staff workers the right kind of physical comfort for maximum efficiency with TRANE Convectors that hug walls, thereby saving management valuable space.

TRANE

THE TRANE COMPANY, LA CROSSE, WIS.
Eastern Mfg. Division . . . Scranton, Penn.
Trane Company of Canada, Ltd. . . . Toronto
OFFICES IN 80 U.S., 14 CANADIAN CITIES

MANUFACTURING ENGINEERS OF HEATING, VENTILATING AND AIR CONDITIONING EQUIPMENT

DISASTERS

QUAKE

A 7.5 earthquake centered in Tehachapi, California is felt throughout the state, as well as Arizona and Nevada. Twelve die, 100,000 square miles are effected and the estimated cost of damages is $50 million in Kern County.

After three crashes in two months, Newark airport is closed down for an investigation and reopens later in the year with a new runway. Following a crash in late 1951, a January crash kills 29 people, both those on board and some living in nearby homes hit by the plane during landing. Less than three weeks later another crash kills 33 on takeoff, including some in an apartment building in the area.

WASHINGTON STATE is the scene of the worst crash in aviation history when over 80 military men die as the plane they are taking home for the Christmas holidays crashes on takeoff.

A FIRE ON THE BOARDWALK

at Atlantic City, New Jersey causes $4 million in damage.

Fires caused by severe drought conditions destroys property in approximately 30 states.

In **CARACAS**, **Venezuela**, 53 church-goers die in a mad dash for the door when pickpockets begin a fire scare.

The entire U.S. is victimized by floods, especially severe in Midwestern and Southern states. An estimated 2-1/2 million acres of crops are destroyed in over 100 cities in 15 states, causing $300 million in damage.

FLOODS

A one-day flood in Southern California leaves 21 dead and 2,000 without homes.

bus

The worst U.S. bus accident ever, a head-on collision between two Greyhound buses in Texas, kills 28 people.

1952

LOCUST INVASION

The worst locust invasion in a century hits Asia, the Middle East and Africa, threatening food supplies in over a dozen countries. With the help of U.S. and Russian planes, insecticides are dropped on infected areas.

A Madrid trolley goes astray and falls into the Manzaneres River, 600 feet below, killing 30 people.

HEAT WAVE

A summertime European heat wave causes the deaths of over 400.

TRAIN CRASHES

 A crash between two express trains and a commuter train kills 112 and injures over 200 in **Middlesex, England**.

In a similar accident near **Rio de Janeiro, Brazil**, two trains collide, killing over 100 people and injuring approximately 200.

A Foggy Day in London Town

Coal combined with sulfur dioxide makes for a deadly fog which kills approximately 4,000 people in the London area. Thousands more have breathing problems.

ZAROUR RIVER

A cloudburst over a small Algerian town causes the Zarour River to rise 18 feet in several moments, killing over two dozen people, livestock and destroying homes.

INDIA

An outbreak of cholera in Calcutta takes the lives of 460.

In the Himalayas, 350 spiritual worshippers lose their lives in a storm.

In the mid-Atlantic, the aircraft carrier "Wasp" smashes into the minesweeper "Hobson," sinking the "Hobson" and drowning 176 of its crew members.

A TYPHOON IN THE PHILIPPINES KILLS OVER 400.

SPORTS 1952

With young stars like **Mickey Mantle** at the plate *(left)* and veterans like **Allie Reynolds** on the mound *(right)* the American League leaders keep a tight grip on their World Series crown.

NEW YORK YANKEES WIN THEIR FOURTH STRAIGHT WORLD CHAMPIONSHIP

Fans go wild as the New York Yankees beat the Brooklyn Dodgers four games to three.

It's their fourth straight world championship under the managerial genius of **Casey Stengel**.

Will Casey *(below)* bring the Yankees to their fifth win next year? Only time will tell.

The Army swears in Dodger pitcher **Don Newcombe**.

Ted Williams hits a game winning two-run home run in his final at-bat before leaving to fight in the Korean War.

Named as Director of Community Activities for NBC's New York stations, Brooklyn Dodger **Jackie Robinson** becomes the first black executive of a major radio or television network. His focus will be delinquency programs for boys.

Appearing on a local New York television show **Jackie Robinson** accuses the Yankee organization of being racist due to its failure to have any black players on its team. Commissioner Ford Frick plans to take action against Robinson.

Larry Doby becomes the first black to win a home run title.

Organized baseball gets its first black umpire—**Emmett L. Ashford**.

Home Run Leaders

National League
Ralph Kiner (Pittsburgh, 37)
Hank Sauer (Chicago, 37)

American League
Larry Doby (Cleveland, 32)

Batting Champions

National League
Stan Musial (St. Louis, .336)

American League
Ferris Fain (Philadelphia, .327)

Most Valuable Player

National League
Hank Sauer (Chicago)

American League
Bobby Shantz (Philadelphia)

Strikeouts

National League
Warren Spahn (Boston, 183)

American League
Allie Reynolds (New York, 160)

Rookie Of The Year

National League
Joe Black (Brooklyn)

American League
Harry Byrd (Philadelphia)

⚾ Shutting out the Detroit Tigers 1-0 in a 12-inning game, 46-year-old **Satchel Paige** becomes the oldest pitcher to complete a major league baseball game.

⚾ Despite a Korean War wage freeze, **Stan Musial** gets a salary increase to $85,000 due to the U.S. Standardization Board which gives its approval to raises for individual players.

⚾ New York Yankee shortstop **Phil Rizzuto** signs a contract for an estimated $45,000 a year.

⚾ $75,000, the second highest salary in the National League, goes to Pittsburgh Pirates outfielder **Ralph Kiner**.

⚾ New York Yankees catcher **Yogi Berra** earns an estimated $37,500.

⚾ The Pittsburgh Pirates set a new precedent becoming the first team to wear helmets which protect the temples.

⚾ In a game against the Cincinnati Reds, the Brooklyn Dodgers break the major league record set in 1901 by scoring 15 runs in the first inning beating the Reds 19-1.

⚾ Calling it a "travesty," head of minor league baseball, **George M. Trautman**, refuses to approve a contract signing 24-year-old Mrs. Eleanor Engle to play ball for the Harrisburg Senators of the Class B Interstate League.

WORLD SERIES
NEW YORK YANKEES OVER BROOKLYN DODGERS, 4-3

All-Star Game
National over American, 3-2
(5 innings due to rain)
Casey Stengel, American Manager
Leo Durocher, National Manager

They Don't Call Him "THE LIP" For Nothing

- *New York Giants manager LEO DUROCHER is fined $100 and suspended for five days for threatening an umpire.*

- *LEO DUROCHER is suspended for four days for arguing with an umpire.*

- *Citing an alleged "bean ball" pitching incident in a Giants-Dodgers game, LEO DUROCHER is fined $100 and suspended for two days.*

- *The New York Giants rehire LEO DUROCHER as manager through 1953.*

No-Hit Game
Carl Erskine: Brooklyn over Chicago, 5-0
Virgil Trucks: Detroit over Washington, 1-0
Detroit over New York, 1-0

WHAT A YEAR IT WAS!

Illustrated above: State Commander 4-door sedan.   Chrome wheel discs optional at extra cost—decorative and other specifications subject to change without notice.

Studebaker again steps out ahead in style!

HERE'S advanced new swept-back styling for discriminating 1952 car buyers.

Here's exciting new aerodynamic designing by Studebaker, the originator of the modern look in cars.

Stop in right away at a nearby Studebaker showroom and arrange to try out one of these thrilling, thrifty, eagerly responsive Studebaker style stars.

Studebaker's the newest of the new for '52—a sprightly new Studebaker Champion in the lowest price field—a brilliant-performing new 120-horsepower Studebaker Commander V-8.

See Studebaker for '52

©1952, Studebaker, South Bend 27, Indiana, U. S. A.

Starring the Starliner—Studebaker's dramatically new and different "hard-top" convertible—Champion or Commander V-8.

161

50,000 football fans show up in Cleveland to see the Detroit Lions get going against the Cleveland Browns in the playoffs for the pro title.

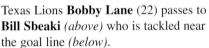

Texas Lions **Bobby Lane** (22) passes to **Bill Sbeaki** *(above)* who is tackled near the goal line *(below)*.

But their hopes are short-lived as there's nothing like a pass interception to slow the opposition down. Cleveland's **Graham** hits his man but it's deflected as **Jim Davis** intercepts, bringing the Lions a big step closer to their first pro title in 17 years.

It's practically clinched when **Doug Walker** of SMU fame breaks loose for the longest play of the game.

On a quarterback sneak Lane bangs the door open and the Lions, though outgained in every department, are never overtaken.

The Browns have won five pro titles and with **Harry Jagate** pulling for yardage, Cleveland rooters take heart that the home team may do it again.

They can't catch him!

It's 67 yards for a touchdown. 17 years is a long time between titles and this is the year the Lions roared.

WHAT A YEAR IT WAS!

NATIONAL FOOTBALL LEAGUE CHAMPIONS

Detroit Lions over **Cleveland Browns**
17-7

ROSE BOWL

Illinois over **Stanford**
40-7

HEISMAN TROPHY

Billy Vessels
Oklahoma, HB

NATIONAL COLLEGE FOOTBALL CHAMPIONS

Michigan State & Georgia Tech

NUMBER ONE DRAFT CHOICE

Bill Wade
QB, Vanderbilt to
Los Angeles Rams

NFL PRO BOWL

National over **American**
30-13

FOOTBALL NEWS

An article published in a Russian newspaper describes American football as a vehicle whose purpose is to teach racist hatred for other people, to prepare U.S. youth for its place in an army of bandits and haters of mankind and to cripple the young both spiritually and physically.

Famous Births

Bill **Walton**	Guillermo **Vilas**
Bob **Costas**	Jimmy **Connors**
Cathy **Rigby**	Lynn **Swann**

1952 BASKETBALL

The basketball scandals of last year are all but forgotten as the Cinderella team from Philadelphia, The **LaSalle Explorers**, capture the hearts of basketball fans in the National Invitation Tournament.

The most underrated quintet of the 12 college teams entered, LaSalle took on the top seated teams and then takes the play away from Dayton in the finals.

A big upset and the biggest story of the year in basketball erupts into jubilation in New York.

NBA ALL-STAR GAME

East
over
West
108-91

NBA CHAMPIONS

Minneapolis Lakers
over
New York Knicks
4-3

NBA SCORING LEADER
season

Paul Arizin
Philadelphia
1,674 points
(25.4 avg.)

NCAA CHAMPIONS

Kansas
over
St. John's
80-63

WHAT A YEAR IT WAS!

BOXING 1952

Rocky MARCIANO DEFEATS "Jersey" Joe WALCOTT

Marciano is knocked down in the first round by the aging **"Jersey" Joe Walcott**.

The 28-year-old ex-GI from Brockton, Massachusetts *(right)* comes back strong in an action-packed 13th round with a right handed jaw crusher knocking out Walcott. It is Rocky's 43rd consecutive victory making him the first unbeaten heavyweight to win the title as well as the first white boxer to win the title since James J. Braddock back in the 1930's.

In the year's most dramatic battle seen coast-to-coast via closed-circuit television in 49 theatres in 31 cities, Rocky Marciano is the new heavyweight champ, the richest crown in boxing.

WHAT A YEAR IT WAS!

HEAVYWEIGHT
"Jersey" Joe Walcott
Rocky Marciano

MIDDLEWEIGHT
Sugar Ray Robinson

WELTERWEIGHT
Kid Gavilan

FEATHERWEIGHT
Sandy Saddler

LIGHTWEIGHT
James Carter
Lauro Salas

LIGHT HEAVYWEIGHT
Joey Maxim
Archie Moore

BOXING NEWS

• Undefeated heavyweight **Rocky Marciano** knocks out **Harry "Kid" Matthews** in 2 mins. 4 secs. of the second round in a match held in New York.

• Ex-champ **Joe Louis** announces he has given up fighting except for exhibition matches.

• One of the few states with a ban on mixed race matches, Florida finally allows an interracial bout between black welterweight champ **Kid Gavilan** and caucasian **Bobby Dykes**.

• With the mercury climbing to 104 degrees, **Sugar Ray Robinson** fails in winning the light-heavyweight crown when the intense heat prevents him from coming out of his corner for the 14th round.

• Japan gets its first world boxing champion when 28-year-old **Yoshiro Shirai** defeats flyweight champ **Dado Marino** of Honolulu.

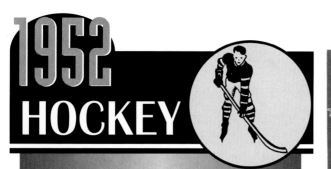

1952 HOCKEY

ALL TIME ALL STARS by Grantland Rice

STANLEY CUP CHAMPIONS

DETROIT RED WINGS
over
MONTREAL CANADIENS,
4-0

ROSS TROPHY
(LEADING SCORER)

GORDIE HOWE, Detroit

VEZINA TROPHY
(OUTSTANDING GOALIE)

TERRY SAWCHUK, Detroit

CALDER MEMORIAL TROPHY
(ROOKIE OF THE YEAR)

"BOOM BOOM" GEOFFRION,
Montreal

LADY BYNG MEMORIAL TROPHY
(MOST GENTLEMANLY PLAYER)
SID SMITH, Toronto

HART MEMORIAL TROPHY (MVP)

GORDIE HOWE, Detroit

Scoring his 325th goal, MAURICE "The Rocket" RICHARD sets a National Hockey League record and the winning puck is sent to Queen Elizabeth II.

RACING'S TOP TEAM...

ARCARO and CITATION

Their Unusual Records

Eddie Arcaro rode Citation in his leading triumphs as a two- and three-year-old. He was in the saddle when this wonder horse won his Triple Crown: Derby, Preakness and Belmont. Arcaro rates as possibly the greatest stake rider of all time. Citation matched Man o' War as a 3-year-old, then set a new world's record mile of 1:33 3/5 in his fifth year. Of racing's many great horse-and-jockey combinations, Arcaro and Citation get my vote as turfdom's ideal all-time team.

Here's another unusual record: 8 of America's top 10 tobacco companies use Atlantic Bond Paper. *Your* business forms and letterheads will look better on clean, crisp, distinctive . . .

ATLANTIC BOND PAPER

A Business

MADE BY EASTERN CORPORATION • BANGOR, MAINE

Write us on your letterhead for Grantland Rice's selections of Turfdom's Greatest Horses, attractively illustrated and suitable for framing.

Day at the DERBY

KENTUCKY DERBY
Hill Gail, *ridden by* **Eddie Arcaro**

PREAKNESS
Blue Man, *ridden by* **Conn McCreary**

BELMONT STAKES
One Count, *ridden by* **Eddie Arcaro**

HORSE OF THE YEAR
One Count
(Daily Racing Form)
Native Dancer
(National Turf Writers Assn.)

MONEY LEADERS
Jockey **Eddie Arcaro**
$1,410,160
Horse **Crafty Admiral**
$277,225

Other ARCARO News

Setting a thoroughbred racing record for American jockeys, in the third race at Chicago's Arlington Park **Arcaro** wins his 3,000th race riding *Ascent* across the finish line.

Arcaro sets a new purse record becoming the first jockey to ride horses winning $2,000,000 in a single year when he rides Calumet Farm's *Mark-Ye-Well* to victory at Belmont.

Fans turn out by the thousands for the annual Kentucky Derby.

This fan studies the racing form to pick a winner.

Patient fans line up and wait their turn at the jammed betting windows.

Four-time Derby winner **EDDIE ARCARO** scores another victory atop *Hill Gail*, the classic colt of Calumet Farm, trotting them both into the Hall of Fame.

WHAT A YEAR IT WAS!

167

1952 Memorial Day At
INDIANAPOLIS

The big day of the year for auto racing in the 500-mile speedway classic on the famous brick track.

Bill Lukovich is leading with only eight laps to go.

Then the checkered flag signals the emergence of a new speedway king, **Troy Ruttman** from Lynwood, California.

The new champ is the youngest and heftiest in the race.

INDIANAPOLIS 500	LE MANS	WINSTON CUP
Troy Ruttman	**Hermann Lang &**	**Tim Flock**
Agajanian Special	**Fritz Reiss**	
128.922 mph	Mercedes-Benz, 96.67 mph	

WHAT A YEAR IT WAS!

BULL FIGHTING

Blonde Texan **PATRICIA McCORMICK** is the first woman from North America to become a bullfighter and makes her debut in Juarez, Mexico where she gets herself two bulls.

RODEO

ALL-AROUND CHAMPION
COWBOY

HARRY TOMPKINS

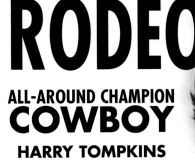

TENNIS

U.S. OPEN	
FRANK SEDGMAN over GARDNAR MULLOY	
MAUREEN CONNOLLY over DORIS HART	
WIMBLEDON	
FRANK SEDGMAN over JAROSLAV DROBNY	
MAUREEN CONNOLLY over LOUISE BROUGH	
DAVIS CUP	
AUSTRALIA over U.S., 4-1	

BOWLING

BPAA ALL-STAR TOURNAMENT

Junie McMahon
Marion Ladewig

AMERICAN BOWLING CONGRESS TOURNAMENT

Al Sharkey

WOMEN'S INTERNATIONAL BOWLING CONGRESS

Lorene Craig

BOWLER OF THE YEAR

Steve Nagy
Marion Ladewig

The American Bowling Congress approves the use of an automatic pinsetter.

1952

70,000 PEOPLE ATTEND THE OPENING OF THE 15TH OLYMPIC GAMES AT HELSINKI

The big story of the summer Olympics is the participation of Russian teams. Along with a temporary smile of good fellowship, they bring their own scoring system.

"We won," they told the home folks. Everybody else knows who really won.

Everyone is busy applauding performers like **Emil Zatopek** of Czechoslovakia, winner of three events in distant racing.

Zatopek's unprecedented triple victory was one of the highlights of the games.

Another stand out thriller is the 100 meter dash, so close the camera had to pick the winner, **Lindy Remigino** of New York.

WHAT A YEAR IT WAS!

TRACK & FIELD

BOSTON MARATHON
Doroteo Flores
Guatemala

After 16 days of competition, Uncle Sam's star spangled athletes achieve their greatest Olympic triumph ever winning 614 points to 553 1/2 for the U.S.S.R.

THE FINAL TALLY
(TOP FIVE COUNTRIES)

MEDALS	TOTAL	GOLD
USA	76	40
USSR	69	21
Hungary	42	16
Sweden	35	12
Italy	21	8

WHAT A YEAR IT WAS!

TRACK & FIELD NEWS

- Scoring 7,825 points in Olympic trials in California, **BOB MATHIAS** breaks his 1950 decathlon record (7,444 points) becoming the first four-time U.S. national decathlon champion.

- In British track & field games in London, American **CHARLES MOORE** sets world record, hurdling 440 yards in 51.6 seconds.

- In the Windsor-to-Chiswick race, Britain's **JIM PETERS** runs the fastest marathon ever recorded — 2 hrs. 20 mins. 42.2 secs.

GOLF

U.S. OPEN	Julius Boros Louise Suggs
PGA	Jim Turnesa
PGA/LPGA LEADING MONEY WINNER	Julius Boros $37,033 Betsy Rawls $14,505
PGA PLAYER OF THE YEAR	Julius Boros
MASTERS	Sam Snead
U.S. AMATEUR	Jack Westland Jacqueline Pung
BRITISH OPEN	Bobby Locke
SENIOR PGA	Ernest Newnham

Boxer **JOE LOUIS** forces a showdown with the PGA's banning of blacks from playing in PGA-sponsored tournaments and becomes the first black to play in a PGA tournament.

Louisville, Kentucky opens its golf courses to blacks.

172

CYCLING

TOUR de FRANCE
Fausto Coppi
Italy

SWIMMING

33-year-old FLORENCE CHADWICK is the first woman to swim the 21-mile Catalina Channel making the swim in 13 hrs. 17 mins.

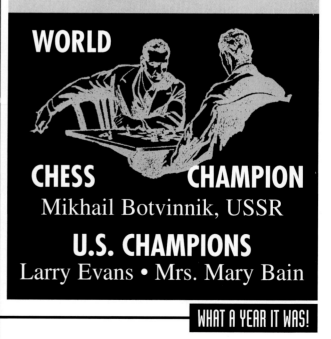

WORLD

CHESS   CHAMPION

Mikhail Botvinnik, USSR

U.S. CHAMPIONS
Larry Evans • Mrs. Mary Bain

WHAT A YEAR IT WAS!

Figure Skating

World Champions

Dick Button
U.S. (5th consecutive year)

Jacqueline du Bief
France

U.S. Champions

Dick Button

Tenley Albright
(7th consecutive year)

Skating News

Two-time Olympic winner **Dick Button** signs a $150,000 contract with Ice Capades of 1953.

Ice-skating champ **Terry Browne** sets a new world jumping record leaping across 15 barrels totaling 28 ft. 3 in. at Grossinger, New York.

DOG SHOW WINNER

WESTMINSTER KENNEL CLUB
Best-In-Show

Rancho Dobe's Storm

Doberman

Roller Derby

The New York Chiefs win the championship for the third time in the four-year history of roller derby's world series competition.

ASSORTED AWARDS

AP ATHLETE OF THE YEAR
Bob Mathias (Track)
Maureen Connolly (Tennis)

JAMES E. SULLIVAN MEMORIAL AWARD
Horace Ashenfelter (Track)

THE HICKOCK BELT
Rocky Marciano (Boxing)

BILLIARDS

Three-Cushion World Title **WILLIE HOPPE**, U.S.

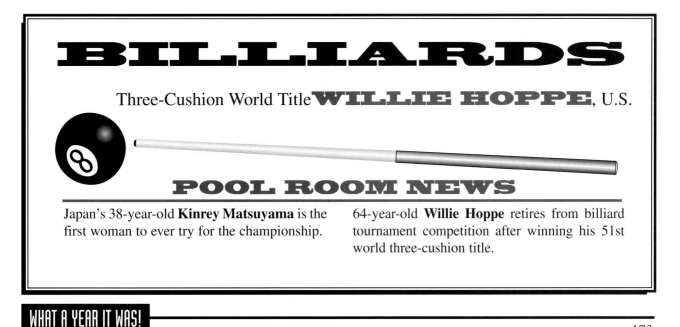

POOL ROOM NEWS

Japan's 38-year-old **Kinrey Matsuyama** is the first woman to ever try for the championship.

64-year-old **Willie Hoppe** retires from billiard tournament competition after winning his 51st world three-cushion title.

1952 WAS A GREAT YEAR, BUT...

THE BEST IS YET TO COME!

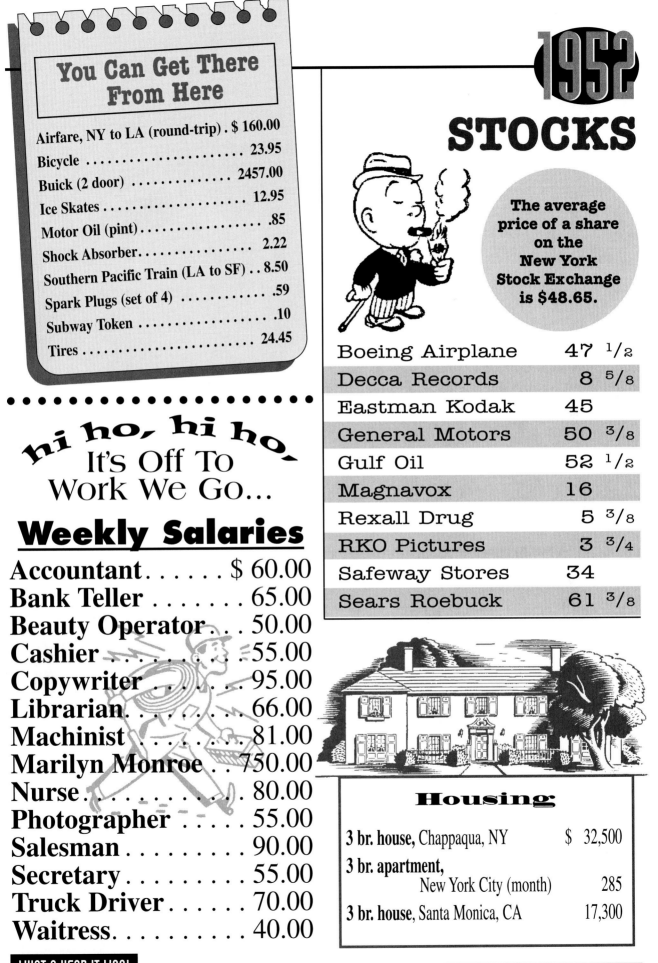

You Can Get There From Here

Airfare, NY to LA (round-trip) . $ 160.00
Bicycle 23.95
Buick (2 door) 2457.00
Ice Skates 12.95
Motor Oil (pint) 85
Shock Absorber 2.22
Southern Pacific Train (LA to SF) . . 8.50
Spark Plugs (set of 4) 59
Subway Token 10
Tires 24.45

hi ho, hi ho, It's Off To Work We Go...

Weekly Salaries

Accountant . . . . . . $ 60.00
Bank Teller 65.00
Beauty Operator . . . 50.00
Cashier 55.00
Copywriter 95.00
Librarian 66.00
Machinist 81.00
Marilyn Monroe . . 750.00
Nurse 80.00
Photographer 55.00
Salesman 90.00
Secretary 55.00
Truck Driver 70.00
Waitress 40.00

1952

STOCKS

The average price of a share on the New York Stock Exchange is $48.65.

Boeing Airplane	47 1/2
Decca Records	8 5/8
Eastman Kodak	45
General Motors	50 3/8
Gulf Oil	52 1/2
Magnavox	16
Rexall Drug	5 3/8
RKO Pictures	3 3/4
Safeway Stores	34
Sears Roebuck	61 3/8

Housing

3 br. house, Chappaqua, NY	$ 32,500
3 br. apartment, New York City (month)	285
3 br. house, Santa Monica, CA	17,300

WHAT A YEAR IT WAS!

155